Greater Manchester MURDERS

ALAN HAYHURST

The History Press

First published 2009
Reprintd 2010

The History Press
The Mill, Brimscombe Port
Stroud, Gloucestershire, GL5 2QG
www.thehistorypress.co.uk

British Library Cataloguing in Publication Data.
A catalogue record for this book is available from the British Library.

ISBN 978 0 7509 5091 6

Typesetting and origination by The History Press
Printed in Great Britain
Manufacturing managed by Jellyfish Print Solutions Ltd

CONTENTS

ALSO BY THE AUTHOR

Cheshire Murders
Lancashire Murders
Staffordshire Murders

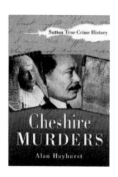  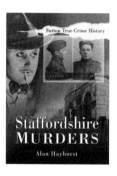

ACKNOWLEDGEMENTS

The author is indebted to and would like to thank the staff of the National Archives, Kew, who as ever, did their very best to be helpful; the staff of Manchester Central Library and Archives; Tameside Local Studies and Archives Centre; Frank Ballington, for a fascinating two-hour conversation, when he gave me the story of his great-grandfather; Kathleen Morris, for help with the Britland case; Alan and Marie Elmer, who first pointed me in the direction of William Robert Taylor and the Manchester Martyrs; Frank R. Marshall & Co., auctioneers, for supplying their photograph of Henry Pierrepoint's hanging book; Stewart Evans; Robert Smith for his kind assistance with illustrations; and Matilda Richards and the team at The History Press.

As ever, I owe a debt of gratitude to my long-suffering wife, who has kept fit by trudging up and down stairs with countless cups of coffee whilst this book was being written.

INTRODUCTION

Greater Manchester is a Metropolitan County in the North-West of England, with a population of approximately 2.6 million. It was created on 1 April 1974 as a result of the Local Government Act 1972 and consists of ten Metropolitan Boroughs: Bolton, Bury, Oldham, Rochdale, Stockport, Tameside, Trafford, Wigan and the cities of Salford and Manchester. There have been several changes to the county over the years, but the citizens of the various boroughs still cling to the old names with considerable pride and indeed many of them still stoutly claim that they are true Lancastrians, the traditional boundaries of Lancashire still being in existence.

Naturally, Manchester itself, the largest of the constituent parts, claims precedence and it is true that the preponderance of wealth and population in the nineteenth and early twentieth centuries resided here. However, there was also considerable poverty and many people in the county lived ten or a dozen to a tiny house, with rudimentary sewage, if any at all. Unemployment was rife and there was little help for the suffering poor.

Hardly surprising, therefore, that the inhabitants of what was to become Greater Manchester went to the bottle for some small comfort, and it was this very liking for strong liquor which was the root cause of many of the murders that took place within its boundaries. Many, of course, were just routine stories of a drunken husband ill-treating his wife, most men having at least one cut-throat razor handy in the house. This type of crime probably accounted for over 70 per cent of all murders committed; these I have tried to ignore.

During my research, I have spent some time at the National Archives, Kew and have been able, under the auspices of the Freedom of Information Act 2000, to inspect several files which have never before been open to the public. The Manchester Central Library has also provided much information, and I have tried to avoid putting words into the mouths of the people mentioned in this book, relying for the most part on verbatim accounts in the newspapers of the time and in the Archive's files. It has also been my good fortune to meet several people whose family were intimately connected with a particular crime and who were good enough to discuss it with me.

1

A MULTIPLE TRAGEDY

Manchester, 1862

On a bitterly cold Sunday 19 January 1862, a tremendous explosion occurred in Great Ducie Street, Strangeways. It was centred on a shop and premises at No. 5, Britannia Buildings, the rented home of William Robert Taylor, who traded as a butter factor and provision dealer. The explosion had been caused by the bursting of the kitchen back-boiler, probably due to the freezing of the cold water pipe. The fire grate and burning coals were flung into the middle of the room, almost covering seven-year-old Maria Jane Taylor, who had been sitting in front of the fire at the time of the explosion. The young girl was terribly injured, having been scalded by the escaping steam and burned by the heated grate and the red-hot ashes. Barely conscious, she was taken to the Manchester Royal Infirmary, where she subsequently died from her injuries.

Her father and step-mother, William Robert and Martha Ann Taylor were out at the time and there are confusing reports as to the injuries of their other three children: Mary Hannah aged twelve, Hannah Maria aged eight and William Robert aged five, but it appears that if any of them were injured, it was only slightly.

Maria Jane was subsequently buried at Harpurhey Cemetery in an unmarked pauper's grave, as the Taylors were unable to afford anything better.

Upon examination, it was found that the brickwork on both sides of the fireplace had been displaced by the force of the blast and the chimney breast had also collapsed. The fireplace of the adjoining property, belonging to a Mr Samuel Hill, had also been forced out and considerable damage done to the room. In both houses, windows were broken by the force of the explosion.

Earlier that month, William Taylor had complained of a leaking pipe, which the landlord's agent gave instructions to be mended, but a few days later, Taylor again reported a leak, which this time seems to have been ignored by the land agent and on the Sunday evening came the dreadful explosion.

The Taylors had first moved into Britannia Buildings in October 1861, paying one quarter's rent in advance, but when time came for the next payment at Christmas, trade was poor and they had not the money to pay it, even though they were threatened with a distress warrant. After the explosion, their position was even more desperate, and according to the neighbours, the family suffered from cold and shortage of food. The tragic death of their child naturally hit the Taylors hard and the business suffered even more. With unseemly haste, bailiffs entered the premises, and took away most of their possessions towards the overdue rent. One report said that the eldest girl was dressing herself at the time and that one of the bailiffs even snatched a comb out of the girl's hand and put it in his pocket.

Some days later, the bailiffs returned and this time took practically everything left in the house, including wet clothes that had been washed and were drying on the line. This barbarous act was believed to have been on the orders of the landlord's agent, Mr Evan Meller, who had his offices in St James's Chambers, South King Street, a four-storey building which no longer exists. The position of William Taylor, his wife and remaining three children can hardly be imagined, their business defunct, their goods seized and now more or less homeless, with no warmth, little food and only the clothes they stood up in.

What is certain is that poor Taylor, half demented from the tragedy, placed the blame for his daughter's death fairly and squarely on Mr Meller, which was hardly surprising, considering the way in which the bereaved family had been treated. For some weeks, he pursued the land agent, claiming compensation for his loss, but his claim was stoutly refuted by Meller, who insisted that the root cause of the explosion was down to Taylor. After some argument, Meller arranged for the premises to be repaired and some weeks later Taylor again fell to arguing with Meller about fixtures

The Taylors, from a contemporary drawing. (Courtesy of Alan and Marie Elmer)

and fittings, for which he had evidently paid £10 when first going into the premises and now felt should be returned to him. This was also stoutly resisted.

On 26 March, the next quarter's rent was due and once again, Taylor did not have the money and although another distress warrant was issued on 30 April, by now there was little or nothing for the bailiffs to seize. It is probable that Mr Meller sent the bailiffs in again with no hope of receiving any money but rather to force the Taylors to leave the premises, promising them that if they did so, he would forgo the rent owing and consider the matter closed. Taylor and his family could hardly have been in any worse condition than the one in which they now found themselves. At least in the workhouse, which was their only other alternative, they would have received some degree of food, clothing and shelter, but Taylor was a stubborn man and insisted on remaining at Britannia Buildings. When the bailiffs arrived yet again, he forcibly ejected them from his premises, but they now had an excuse to force themselves and, ignoring the protestations of Taylor and his distraught wife, they stormed back in and took away the last few remaining sticks of furniture.

Over the next few weeks, the Taylors clung grimly to their now empty property, expecting a further visit from the bailiffs at any moment. On several occasions, Taylor went to Meller's office, where he was usually seen by the land agent's nineteen-year-old son, William, to whom he complained that the bailiffs had pocketed various items for themselves and that the rest of the goods taken had been sold under value. Young Meller protested that there was nothing that he could do and noted that Taylor did not lose his temper, or appear to be any sort of threat when these conversations took place.

On 16 May, William Meller arrived for work at around 9 a.m., some minutes before his father, and was closely followed into the office by William Taylor, accompanied by his wife. The offices, which were on the second floor of the building and reached by a winding staircase, consisted of a general and a private office, plus a small ante-room. The Taylors, finding that Mr Meller senior had not yet arrived, sat down in the ante-room, arranging themselves in such a position that William Taylor could see clearly the entrance to the premises and the stairway, whilst his wife looked towards the inner offices. A few minutes later, Evan Meller arrived and, seeing the Taylors waiting there, greeted them courteously enough.

However, William Meller who was in the private office, suddenly heard words and saw his father struggling in the grip of William Taylor, crying 'Oh. Mr Taylor.' Taylor appeared to be striking at the land agent, although young Meller could not see clearly with what. Hurrying to help his father, the boy was suddenly confronted by Mrs Taylor, who produced a revolver, which she pointed at him. Greatly alarmed, William dashed back into the private office and slammed the door behind him. For some minutes, he remained there, frightened to confront the Taylors again. He then heard the report of a pistol.

Venturing out into the general office, he was relieved to see that the Taylors appeared to have gone and he moved carefully towards the staircase, when to his great concern, he saw his father's body lying on the first-floor landing, bleeding from the mouth.

One of the other tenants in the building, a Mr Leatherbrow, had appeared, having heard the commotion, accompanied by a porter named Hooley, and the two men had knelt by the fallen Meller, just as William Taylor reappeared waving the revolver. This had gone off with a loud report and wounded the porter in the knee. With a cry, Hooley had slumped against the wall, clutching his leg, then clawed his way upright and limped off down the stairs.

The noise of the gunshot attracted a third man, Mr Pankhurst, who arrived just as the young William Meller dashed down the stairs to comfort his father. Taylor immediately pointed his revolver at the boy, causing him to draw back behind the others present.

Pankhurst, showing not a little bravery, confronted Taylor and asked him angrily, 'Good God, what do you mean by this?'

Taylor muttered, 'He has ruined me and my children,' at which Pankhurst turned back to attend to the recumbent Meller, who was still showing signs of life. Without saying anything more, William Taylor turned on his heel and dashed down the stairs to the street door, where his wife was waiting for him.

The others now tried to make Meller as comfortable as possible and in due course, the injured man was taken to the infirmary. It was found that he had suffered no fewer than eleven stab wounds to the body, one of which had penetrated the heart and another the chest, either of which was bad enough to prove fatal. Nothing could be done for him and he died shortly after reaching the hospital.

In the meantime, young Meller had run out of the building and gone to the nearby police station. Breathlessly telling his story, he accompanied a police officer back to the offices, where they saw Mrs Taylor near the entrance, together with her husband, still holding the revolver. This time, William Taylor offered no resistance when the police constable gingerly removed the weapon from his hand, but muttered words to the effect that Evan Meller had murdered his children. Whilst he was being searched, he said, 'Thank God, my work is done.'

As a result of the search, Taylor was found to have on him a bullet mould, a powder flask, some percussion caps, and a paper sheath which appeared to be for a knife. The knife was later found on the landing where the struggle had taken place. The revolver was proved to have been bought, together with the bullet mould, from a nearby store and it was a rather old fashioned weapon, having six barrels which all revolved together. On inspection, it was found that one barrel had been discharged.

During questioning at the police station, Taylor pulled from his waistcoat pocket a ring bearing three keys, which he told the police were for a bedroom at Britannia Buildings, 'Where,' he said, 'you will find something.' When the police reached Britannia Buildings, they found the place in great disorder: the walls and staircase daubed with black and what little remained of the contents of the house smashed to pieces. On the floor was a large piece of marble slab, which had been taken from the fireplace and, to their horror, the police found the bodies of three

The murder scene. (Courtesy of Alan and Marie Elmer)

The Scene of the Murder of Mr. Meller.

children laying side by side, their heads on the slab. Each child was naked except for a man's shirt and each had around the neck a black ribbon, with similar pieces around the waist and wrist. Upon the breast of each child was a paper upon which was written:

> We are six; one at Harptry (Harpurhey) lies and thither our bodies take. Meller and son are our cruel murderers, but God and our loving parents will avenge. Love rules here; we are all going to our sister, to part no more.

On the other side of the papers was the name of each child and their ages. On the youngest child, the paper also said, 'Meller our sister slew, through gross neglect.' The bodies of the three children were eventually buried at Harpurhey, in an unmarked pauper's grave.

Taylor was charged with the murder of his three children, remaining silent to the indictment. Sergeant Bateman then turned to the woman, who agreed that she was Taylor's wife, but had nothing further to say. On returning to the police station (the Taylors were taken separately) Mrs Taylor said to PC Hodgson, 'I am come to give myself up.'

The murder scene. (Courtesy of Alan and Marie Elmer)

'What for?' asked Hodgson.

'A man was shot. It is me that has committed the murder of the man.' she said, and showing her wrist to the constable he saw that it had blood on it. She continued, 'It is not the man that they have taken that has done it.'

It is clear that at this time Mrs Taylor was confused; hardly surprising considering the dreadful ordeal she had just suffered. She did not seem to be aware that Mr Meller had been stabbed to death, not shot, whereas the man who had been shot, Hooton, was still alive.

Taylor and his wife appeared at the City Magistrate's Court, an event that was avidly followed by a huge crowd. To prevent any problems during the hearing, the police had issued admission tickets, about 700 in number, which were snapped up within a day. Several thousand more might have been issued if there had been sufficient space in the court, such was the interest. After five hours of evidence, the Taylors were remanded at Kirkdale Gaol to await trial at Liverpool Assizes, accused of the murder of Evan Meller.

The prisoners were taken to Victoria railway station in a police van, which had been driven at a furious pace to the Magistrate's Court, stopping at the magistrate's private entrance to take the prisoners on board, thus foiling the main part of the crowd who were at the rear of the court building where prisoners were more usually dealt with. At the railway station, no attempt was made to keep back the huge crowd that had gathered and many people clambered upon the roof, steps and sides of the second-class carriage in which the prisoners and their escort were confined. Indeed, so many people were clinging to the outside of the train that it was forced to leave the station at a very slow rate until the last of the hangers-on had dropped off as the train finally began to pick up speed.

On Tuesday 20 May, Evan Meller was buried at Chorlton-cum-Hardy Parish Church, the streets being lined with onlookers and on Saturday 31 May the *Manchester Courier* reported that the police had just announced that William Taylor and his 'wife' were not married, although it is not clear whether this information was fact or mere speculation. Whilst the Taylors were being held, their three dead

Kikdale Gaol, c. 1880. (Author's collection)

children were given a big funeral, courtesy of Manchester businessmen, the road to the cemetery being crowded with onlookers. They lie today at Harpurhey, in an unmarked grave.

The trial opened on Thursday 21 August 1862 at the imposing St Georges Hall, Liverpool, before Mr Baron Wilde. Although the judge had given instructions that there was to be no undue publicity about the case, the approaches to the hall were thronged with sightseers and the courtroom was packed to capacity. Twenty-seven years later, the notorious poisoner, Mrs Florence Maybrick, was to be tried in the same courtroom. Appearing for the prosecution were Mr Monk QC, Mr Sowler QC, and Mr Holker; appearing for Taylor were Mr S. Pope QC, and Mr Edwards, with Mr W. Overend QC, and Mr S. Temple appearing for Mrs Taylor.

Taylor and his wife were put up and those in the crowded courtroom noted that they looked well and were of respectable appearance. The accused man had a dark complexion, with very dark hair, moustache and beard, giving him a foreign appearance, whilst his good-looking wife had fair hair and was wearing a plain black bonnet, sporting a large feather and a veil, which she had also worn for the magistrate's hearing. The judge motioned that she could sit down through the hearing and a chair was given to her. Those who had been at the Magistrate's Court noticed that she had changed her hair style.

When called upon to plead, Taylor said in a loud voice, 'Not a shadow of guilt' and his wife said quietly, 'Not guilty.' Mr Monk then opened the prosecution's case by exhorting the jury to put from their minds anything that they might have read in the papers about the affair and to judge the case only on the evidence that would be put before them. He then began to recount the events of 16 May onwards and came eventually to the discovery of the bodies of the three children at Britannia Building:

> How long or by what means these children came by their deaths in the first place, it is no part whatever of our duty to inquire, but they had evidently been washed and laid out. Each child had on it a piece of paper, in handwriting that I believe I shall be able to show is that of the accused, William Robert Taylor. As to motive for an act of so much violence, so desperately perpetrated and so deplorable in its consequences, I suggest that these prisoners were influenced by a passion as strong as any which influences the human mind.

He then impressed on the jury that according to the law, if two people combined in an act of violence in which a person was killed, then both were equally guilty of murder, no matter who administered the fatal blow.

William Galloway Meller then told the court of the attack on his father and that after the gunshot, he had run to the local police station and had returned with a constable to find the accused couple still on the premises and his father mortally injured. Under cross-examination he was definite that Mrs Taylor had menaced him with the gun and that he had seen the barrels clearly.

The wine merchant, Joseph Leatherbrow also gave his story and stated that on seeing Mr Meller, he called his porter, Hooley and together, they wrested the injured man into a sitting position. Whilst the two were holding him in that position, Taylor came down the stairs holding a revolver, which he pointed at Mr

Harpurhey Cemetery, where the Taylor children were buried in unmarked graves. (© A. Hayhurst)

Meller's head and fired. The shot hit the unfortunate Hooley in the arm, passing through the limb and into his knee, and he staggered off down the stairs saying, 'Mr Joseph, I am shot.'

Leatherbrow then said to Taylor, 'What does this mean?' and Taylor replied, 'Oh, he has murdered my children.' In response to further questioning, Leatherbrow stated that at that time, Taylor could have got away if he had wanted to but appeared to have made no effort to escape. Leatherbrow was followed into the witness box by Mr H.F. Pankhurst, whose story tallied almost word for word with the earlier witnesses.

Next to appear was the police surgeon, Mr William Heath, who observed that when he inspected the body of Evan Mellor, he found eleven cut wounds on it, one wound on the right side being about 2½in in length, and passing through the breast bone and the heart. Another wound, which was about 4in deep, passing through the heart, would have required considerable force to make. Sergeant Thomas Bramhall then gave evidence of arrest and also of the discovery of the knife in Meller's office, which Taylor had thrown down.

Mr Thomas Green Jones, a general dealer, said that on 13 May, a man came to his shop at 175 Deansgate and wanted to purchase a revolver. He chose one costing 20s, but had not the money to pay for it. Instead, he offered a watch that Jones accepted in payment and also threw in a bullet mould.

John Maclean, a bailiff, said that he attended the second distress at Taylor's premises and used a hammer to break in the door. They found hardly anything left in the premises, apart from some bread and butter! They stripped the premises of what little there was but did not receive sufficient to satisfy the warrant. There may well have been many in the courtroom who had cause to know just how harsh was the lot of a debtor in mid-Victorian days, and the sympathy that went out from the public gallery to the accused couple was tangible. It was clear to all that the Taylors had been reduced to absolute and irredeemable poverty, with no thought for them or their three young children.

Mr Pope then addressed the court on behalf of Taylor and stood up knowing that he had an almost impossible task to carry out. Clear evidence had been given to the court of Taylor's part in the death of Evan Meller and Pope told the court that he felt almost overborne with the responsibility that now fell on his shoulders. He went on, 'The question I must ask you to decide is this simple and distinct question – was this man conscious, at the time when he committed the act, of the quality and nature of the act that he was doing?'

To establish a defence on the grounds of insanity, it had to be clearly proved that at the time of committing the act, the accused was labouring under such a defect of reason, from disease of the mind, as not to know the nature and quality of the act he was doing, or if he did know it, he did not know that it was wrong. The McNaghten Rules, which remained in force until late in the twentieth century, were formulated after Daniel McNaghten killed Prime Minister Robert Peel's private secretary, in mistake for him, in 1843.

Pope then began an impassioned appeal to the jury to remember the great strain that had been put upon William Taylor and his wife after the death of their young daughter; the first distress levied against them within a week of that event and the second distress that had left them with virtually nothing, even their bed and a single chair had been taken, rendering them utterly destitute. Pope's speech was, at this stage, interrupted for several minutes due to William Taylor suddenly collapsing and falling insensible to the floor of the dock. Whilst he was being attended to, his wife covered her face in her hands and wept, but eventually, Taylor recovered and on the judge's instruction, was also given a chair in the dock.

Pope continued, emphasising that when Taylor assaulted Mr Meller, he was possessed by an all-absorbing delusion which only released its hold on him once he thought that Meller was dead. After that, he said, Taylor reverted to a more normal mien and was content to say, 'He has murdered my children.' Counsel continued:

> I am not sure that in asking you for a verdict of 'not guilty' on the grounds of insanity, I am asking you for a merciful verdict. If that is what your verdict is, he must spend the rest of his days in a penal asylum. I ask you simply to say that for this act, he was not responsible, because he was not of sound mind.

Mr Overend then addressed the court on behalf of Taylor's wife. He had, he said, looked through the evidence for any expression of anger on her part which might indicate that she had any motive for the murder of Mr Meller and it was clear that whatever animosity might have been entertained by her husband, she had entertained none. She went to Meller's office carrying a basket containing two combs, two brushes and a sponge. Whoever heard of a woman setting out to commit a deliberate murder armed thus? Could anyone believe that if she had gone there for a deadly purpose, or had known that her husband had deadly weapons upon him, she could have sat quietly and composed in the office whilst she and her husband waited for Mr Meller to arrive? Taylor had bought the revolver on his own and there was no evidence to show that she knew that he had it. Evidence as to her conduct had been given by young Meller, who had seen his father attacked and killed and by Hooley, who having received a wound was as much in a stage of agitation as was young Meller. It was quite clear from her conversation with the policeman that she did not know how Mr Meller came to his death, but innocent as she was, she was quite willing to sacrifice her life for her husband. Switching tack, he then went on:

> There was nothing whatever to connect her in any way with the deaths of the three children. Whilst the handwriting on the notes was not that of her husband, it was not pretended that it was hers.

No satisfactory explanation as to who actually wrote the note was ever given to the court. He besought the jury to come to such a conclusion that would not only give them satisfaction now, but also raise no qualms later on and that their verdict would be consistent with justice, reason and mercy.

Mr Baron Wilde commenced his summing up by telling the jury to disregard much of what had been said to them in the way of appeals to their passions. The fact of the murder of Evan Meller had been proved beyond a doubt. The prisoners were man and wife, but the jury must consider their guilt separately. It was the husband's act that killed Mr Meller. He stabbed him eleven or twelve times with a knife and then fired a pistol at him and the jury had been invited to consider that he was insane. 'To be sure,' said the judge, 'he never showed himself as insane. No single act had been proved in evidence which was otherwise the act of a sane man and there was no want of health spoken to by any medical man.'

Then came the words that most assuredly settled the fate of William Taylor:

> Therefore the case of insanity, as regards Taylor, was a case in which a man, perfectly sane on all other occasions, with a calm demeanour, with a settled purpose, without any extravagant excitement or any peculiar circumstances surrounding the act, took a knife and stabbed another man twelve times, causing his death.

None of the rest of the summing up carried the same force as those words. In referring to Mrs Taylor, the judge said that the evidence against her was by no means so full and rested chiefly on the one act sworn to by Meller's son, the raising of the pistol. If after hearing the evidence and the summing up, the jury thought that she was taking part in the murder, they must do their duty honestly and fearlessly, but if on the other hand they had a reasonable doubt in her joining in the act, they must give her the benefit of that doubt.

The jury retired at twenty past two and in less than thirty minutes, returned with a 'Guilty' verdict on Taylor and 'Not Guilty' on his wife, who was at once released. The judge then read the death sentence in the usual form, which the prisoner heard with no emotion, except perhaps for a little twitching of the fingers as he clutched the dock rail.

The date of execution was set for 20 September at Kirkdale Prison and Taylor was to be hanged with a convicted Luddite, a man named John Ward, who had been involved in a scuffle with police when attempting to destroy a quantity of man-made bricks at Ashton-under-Lyne, during which PC William Jump was shot and killed. Ward had been convicted with one Burke, a fellow member of the Brickmaker's Trades Union which was violently opposed to their wares being made mechanically. Burke had, however, been reprieved, leaving his comrade to face the death penalty alone.

As was usual for the times, the event was to be a public hanging on a scaffold that was erected at the back of Kirkdale Gaol. The crowd was immense, and many people, unable to afford the train fare, had walked during the night from Ashton, Manchester, Oldham and other places. Excursion trains were continually arriving during the early part of the morning and hundreds of people had been left standing at Oldham station as there was no room for them on the train. On the preceding day, two long beams had been drawn out of 'portholes,' just below an iron door, set high in the north-west angle of the prison wall. On this foundation was then bolted wooden flooring and below the floor was draped a black curtain, which would conceal for the most part the bodies of the men as they hung for the statutory one hour after execution.

On the morning before his death, Taylor had written two letters, one to his wife and the other to his sister in Somerset. The one to his wife said:

> My loving and beloved wife, I woke this morning in peace and quiet. I feel truly peaceful and have no fear of death. I have not one nerve of my whole system in the last state of excitement. Thank you for your letter of yesterday, it was a source of comfort to me. May God give you grace to carry out your good resolutions to the end of time.

The letter went on at some length, exhorting his wife to be a blessing to the family and to lead them in the path of virtue. (It was perhaps an indication of exactly how much strain he was feeling, that he did not seem to realise now that all their children were dead.) In the same envelope, he sent to his wife a lock of hair. The letter concludes:

> Now my dear wife, farewell, farewell to the end of time, but may we meet again. God bless you all. I bid you all farewell and send with all love, my very dear and affectionate wife, your loving and affectionate husband, William Taylor.

At a few minutes past noon, after having had the sacrament administered to them, the two condemned men appeared on the scaffold, accompanied by the executioner Calcraft and the chaplain, the Revd Mr Appleton. The culprits were carefully placed in their correct positions, Taylor on the right-hand side of the spectators and Ward on the left. Whilst the cap was being drawn over Taylor's head, it became clear that he was attempting to speak, but was persuaded or prevented from doing so by the executioner, who pulled the cap over his face and adjusted the rope. After giving Ward similar attention, Calcraft stepped back to pull the lever that would send the two murderers to their doom. Just before he did so, Taylor was heard to exclaim, 'Lord, have mercy on me, Amen.' and then the trap fell. A deep moan came from the huge crowd as the men went to their doom. According to the *Manchester Courier*, both men died without a struggle and if so, they were lucky, as Calcraft was well known for bungling his executions and leaving his victims strangling on the rope.

An hour was allowed to go by and the executed men were then taken down and after a plaster cast had been made of Taylor's face, the two bodies were buried within the prison precincts. Kirkdale Gaol was originally built in 1821 and was eventually sold to Liverpool Corporation in 1894 and demolished. The bodies of sixty-six murderers were removed at that time and buried in a public cemetery in an unmarked grave.

2

THE MANCHESTER MARTYRS

Manchester, 1867

The early part of the nineteenth century was a time of great unrest in Ireland. From the time of Cromwell, much of the land had been confiscated from native Irish Catholics and handed over to absentee English landlords who were almost always far more concerned about their rents than the well-being of their tenants. The Irish peasantry were dependent on the potato crop, and many of them lived on little else, with an acre of land producing up to twelve tons of potatoes, enough to feed a family of six for a year. Even so they lived at subsistence level and could be ejected from their hovels at a moment's notice, on the whim of their landlords. These conditions were a breeding ground for revolution and over the years the Irish rose time and again against their English overlords. However, these affairs were always put down with some savagery by the British militia, who numbered about 100,000 in Ireland by the middle of the nineteenth century.

To add to the Irish troubles, the potato harvest failed in September 1845, turning the crop to an evil smelling mush and rendering it totally uneatable. During three out of the next four years, this tragedy was repeated, leaving many of the Irish peasantry starving, a problem with the British government found difficult to solve. Thousands of starving Irish fled the land of their birth, with many of them going to America to seek a better life and, by 1859, Irishmen and their families accounted for almost 50 per cent of the foreign-born population of the USA.

About this time, a young man by the name of James Stephens founded a secret society which he called the Irish Republican Brotherhood (an early forerunner of the IRA). This soon became known as the Fenian Movement, derived from the Fianna Eirann, a legendary band of Irish warriors led by Fin MacCoul. The object of the Fenians was to overthrow British rule in Ireland and it was their basic belief that this would be impossible to do by political means alone: armed insurrection, they believed, was the only solution.

The Fenians were formed into 'Circles,' the man in charge being known as the 'Centre.' Each Centre had under his control up to nine Sub-Centres, who in turn commanded nine sergeants, each of whom looked after nine privates. At full strength, a Circle would have 820 men, although this figure was rarely reached in practice. A man called John O'Mahoney, who had assisted Stephens with the formation of the Brotherhood, was the 'Head Centre' of the American movement, whilst Stephens held that title for Ireland.

Fenian attempts at armed insurrection were always beaten down by the militia, due in some part to a British Government spy in the offices of the *Irish People*, the official organ of the Fenians, started by Stephens, who acted as Editor in Chief. The paper was allowed to flourish unchallenged in its early days, but on 15 September 1865, their Dublin offices were raided and several Fenian leaders, including Stephens, were arrested. However, within a few days, Stephens had made a daring breakout from Richmond Prison and so avoided the heavy custodial sentences handed down to his colleagues. By 1866, Stephens was in Paris, where he remained for many years, earning a precarious living as a teacher of English.

Meanwhile, the British Government had spies and informers everywhere. In the National Archives at Kew, there are seven thick files bursting with communications from England, Ireland and America, all dealing with the comings and goings of the Fenians. A typical letter, from E.M. Archibald in New York, dated 6 March 1865, says:

> There is continued activity in the proceedings of the Fenian Brotherhood, openly held. Report says there are as many as 10,000 stand of arms in this city. Fully believe that an attempt at insurrection in Ireland will be made in the coming spring.

Another missive to the Home Office informed of a Fenian conspiracy at Liverpool docks, where more than 3,000 Irishmen were employed, whilst a letter from Fleetwood disclosed that a crate containing arms, plus bullets and bullet moulds, had been seized by the Coast Guard at Morecambe on 1 February 1886, *en route* for Dublin.

By 1866, there was a considerable agitation amongst the Brotherhood for another uprising and early in 1867, one took place in Ireland, which the militia again smothered with little difficulty. Stephens, in Paris, was in no position to help and indeed seemed strangely reluctant to do anything at all. Although he still carried the title of Head Centre, he seemed a spent force and was no longer highly regarded by many of the Fenians. His position was eventually taken over in December 1866 by an Irish American, a veteran of the American Civil War, Colonel Thomas J. Kelly, originally from Galway. He had, as his second in command, Captain Timothy Deasy, also a war veteran. Kelly was a strongly built man of medium height, but of the two, it was Deasy, some 4in taller, who had the military bearing.

There were, by now, a number of Civil War veterans in Great Britain, including Captain Edward O'Meagher Condon, who came to Manchester in 1867 to rejuvenate the nine Circles there and who was soon *de facto* Head Circle for the north of England. In charge of the south of England was Captain Ricard O'Sullivan Burke, another Civil War veteran. Condon soon had the Manchester Circles licked into shape and in August 1867, organised a convention, attended by Fenians from all over the country, including Kelly, Deasy, and O'Sullivan Burke. Kelly was now confirmed in his position as Chief Executive of Ireland and it was also decided that another, larger convention must be held in the near future, at which representatives of the whole organisation would gather.

One evening in September, Condon came across two policemen in the company of an Irishman named Corydon, a man who was known to be a police spy acting for the British. Condon therefore decided to send out a message to the Manchester Centres and their Sub-Centres, via one William Melvin, warning them about the presence of the informer in their city.

When Melvin got to the house of one of the Sub-Centres, a man named O'Bolger, he found the house crowded with people he did not know and being well aware of the possibility of betrayal, he decided not to seek out O'Bolger, but instead went next door to his brother, and gave him the message. O'Bolger evidently regarded this as an intentional slight and sought out Condon, complaining bitterly and insisting that he should be allowed to deliver his grievances in person to Colonel Kelly. Condon's first reaction was to tell O'Bolger to concentrate on the matters in hand and stop wasting everyone's time, but O'Bolger made such a fuss of his imagined grievance that Condon decided, for the sake of peace, to give in to his request.

The local Centres met, together with Kelly and Deasy and other Fenians to consider O'Bolger's complaint, although Condon was absent as he had a prior meeting to attend in Birmingham. The outcome is not clear, but it is likely that the meeting dismissed O'Bolger's complaints as irrelevant. Afterwards, Kelly and Deasy left for another meeting at a house in Oak Street, off Shudehill, where Condon had at one time lodged. As they approached the door, they attracted the attention of a passing constable, who hung about in the shadows to see what would happen. He saw Kelly knock on the door and give a sign, after which the door opened and the two men went in. This whetted the constable's curiosity and attracting the attention of Sergeant Brears and another constable, they awaited events in the shadows.

Some minutes later, a man came out to make sure the coast was clear, followed by Kelly and Deasy with two others and at that moment, Sergeant Brears and his constables pounced. As Brears approached, Deasy drew a pistol, but this was wrestled from him before he had a chance to use it. Kelly, too, was overwhelmed before he could use his revolver and was taken, with his companion, to the nearest police station. The other two men managed to get away in the confusion.

The next morning, Kelly and Deasy, giving their names as Wright and Williams, were put up at the city police court, where they claimed that they were American citizens and demanded to be set free. Despite the likelihood that they would be stopped by the police from time to time, especially as they both had pronounced Irish-American accents, they seem to have taken no trouble at all to rehearse themselves a believable story. When Kelly was asked, by the magistrate, where he lived, he replied, 'Nowhere.'

'Then where did you live before?' asked the magistrate, somewhat irritated at Kelly's flippant manner.

'London,' was the reply.

'For how long?'

'Two months.'

'Where before that?'

'America.'

'Do you remember the name of the ship you came over in?'

'No.'

When it came to Deasy's turn, he was equally evasive. 'What have you been doing in this country?' asked the magistrate.

'Nothing.'

'How have you lived?'

'I brought money with me.'

'What vessel did you sail on?'

'I can't remember.'

'What was the name of the Captain?'

'I was a steerage passenger and had little to do with the Captain.'

Kelly and Deasy did themselves no favours with these odd, evasive answers and the magistrate had no compunction in remanding them in custody for a week. 'I suppose there's no possibility of bail?' asked Deasy cheekily. The magistrate frowned, 'None whatsoever.'

Next morning, when Condon returned from his meeting in Birmingham, he was given the shock news that Kelly and Deasy were in the hands of the police and that it would not be long before the authorities discovered who these men really were. Condon immediately called a meeting of the local Centres to consider how best to proceed. Assuming that the two Irish leaders would be remanded in custody after their Magistrate's Court appearance, Condon reasoned that the only way to rescue them would be by waylaying the police van taking them from the court to Belle Vue Prison (approximately on the site of the modern day pleasure grounds) on the Hyde Road.

On the following day, Condon sent one of his men, William Darragh, to Birmingham to buy revolvers from a Fenian sympathiser. To get these, it had been necessary to have a whip-round and when it was found that the local Circle had only £1 in its coffers, an appeal was made amongst other local Circles and enough was raised to buy ten pistols, with which Darragh eventually returned.

Meanwhile, Colonel Ricard O'Sullivan Burke journeyed to Manchester from London and he and Condon met to consider the way forward. It was decided to issue the guns to men chosen by the local Centres, who knew their men much better than they did and amongst their number were William Phillip Allen, Michael Larkin and Captain Michael O'Brien, another Civil War veteran. The pistols were handed out with instructions that they were not to be fired unless it became clear that the venture was about to fail, in which case they were to be used without compunction.

The plan was that Colonel Burke would attend the Magistrate's Court the next morning, when Kelly and Deasy were due to appear, and assuming that they would again be remanded in custody, the prisoners would be taken to Belle Vue Prison, a three-mile journey from the City centre. Just 300yds short of the prison, the London & North Western Railway crossed the Hyde Road by means of a bridge consisting of three arches, the main one over the roadway and a smaller one on either side which allowed pedestrians to pass through. It was to be at this spot that the van would be stopped and the prisoners released, being spirited away over the adjacent brickfields to the Ashton Road. Captain Michael O'Brien was to be the last man away, with the responsibility of seeing that no one followed the escaping men.

On the following morning, Kelly and Deasy arrived at the court and were immediately confronted with the information that the police were now certain as to their proper identities and the fact that they were Fenian leaders. After a short hearing, they were removed to the cells to await the journey to Belle Vue Prison, but by mid afternoon, when the Black Maria (a stout wooden horse-drawn van) arrived, there was a considerable crowd, many of them Irishmen, milling about in the street outside the courthouse.

Condon had despatched two of his men with instructions to keep a watch for Kelly and Deasy and then to hurry back up the Hyde Road, once the Black Maria set off. One of these men, a somewhat unstable 'public lecturer' named John Francis McAuliffe, stood outside the court on the opposite side of the road and, for reasons best known to himself, drew attention to himself by strutting up and down, whistling Fenian songs and grimacing in the most fearful way. Though McAuliffe must have known that he now had the close attention of several policemen, he continued his pantomime until Inspector Garner and PC Shaw approached him. McAuliffe immediately drew a dagger from his pocket, which Garner attempted to wrest from his grasp. Several constables joined in and a fearful melee ensued, during which a punch aimed at Garner hit PC Shaw squarely in the eye, giving him a noticeable 'Badge of honour' for several days afterwards. At last, the burly Irishman was subdued and taken down to the cells. Quite why McAuliffe acted in this way is not clear, but he was almost certainly acting under the influence of alcohol or drugs and his actions were to have an important affect on the plot to free the Fenian leaders.

When the prisoners were brought out, there was still a considerable crowd in front of the courthouse and it required a number of policemen to clear the way. The police van had a door at the rear, which opened to reveal a narrow corridor, on each side of which were a row of separate cells, each designed to hold one prisoner.

Normally, the van was accompanied by only two policemen, who both rode on the outside of the van at the rear, and the plotters had decided that there would be little or no resistance when the van was stopped. However, McAuliffe's antics and the presence of such a large crowd of rowdy onlookers outside the court had persuaded the authorities to reinforce the personnel travelling with the van, which now not only had five policemen, unarmed except for their night-sticks, riding on the back, but Sergeant Charles Brett travelling inside with the prisoners. Following behind was a cab containing another four unarmed policemen, which was to follow the van to Belle Vue Prison.

Kelly and Deasy, both manacled at the wrists, were placed in the farthest cells at the end of the van, facing one another. Another ten prisoners followed, plus two young boys who were being taken to the reformatory and three women, who were considered no danger and were not manacled.

Sergeant Charles Brett, born in Cheshire in 1815, had joined the Manchester Police Force in 1846, being promoted to sergeant, 'E' Division, six years later. His duties were concerned mainly with the transport of prisoners to and from the courts and as such he was well known to many of the criminal fraternity in Manchester. A married man with three children, living in a comfortable terraced house off the Oldham Road, Brett had a good head of hair, wore a neatly trimmed beard and was proud of his appearance in the eight-buttoned police overcoat with the 'E 1' collar markings. He was considered to be firm, but fair in his dealings with prisoners and was known to many of them as 'Charlie.'

At half past three, the van, with its accompanying policemen, started out for Belle Vue, but meanwhile, at the Hyde Road bridge, Condon was having trouble with his fellow plotters. Originally, there were to be just ten, but word of the enterprise had obviously leaked out and there were now about forty Irishmen standing around the arches, drawing the attention of the locals to themselves and generally creating a nuisance. Thinking on his feet, Condon handed out money and told the men to go in to the local beer houses until they were needed, a risky strategy but all he could think of. Several Irish women who had appeared on the scene were taken off to a nearby café and given a meal to keep them quiet. Meanwhile, the local inhabitants looked on curiously.

Colonel O'Sullivan Burke arrived back from the courthouse and had an urgent conversation with Condon. Soon, in the distance, the Black Maria could be seen approaching and the plan was that the attackers would hide in and around the arches of the bridge and at a given signal, launch themselves at the van, break open the rear door, free Kelly and Deasy and then spirit them across open fields on the left and on to the Ashton road, where Condon had arranged for a cab to be waiting to take the fugitives to a safe house in Ashton-under-Lyne.

The van approached and as the horses emerged from underneath the central arch, two men ran into the road and made a grab for them. These were Captain Michael O'Brien and the thirty-two-year-old, scrawny and rather ill-looking Michael Larkin, both waving pistols. Despite Condon's strict orders, shots were fired immediately, and one of the two horses was hit in the neck, forcing the van to a halt. Immediately, a mass of Irishmen attacked the van, two of them climbing up on to the top of the van, where they were handed up heavy stones from the roadside. They then proceeded to try to smash the roof and thus gain entrance. While all this was going on, several more shots were fired, one of them hitting an onlooker named Sprosson in the foot, whilst PC Seth Bromley was wounded in the thigh.

After the fusillade of shots and volleys of stones, the unarmed policemen had fallen back, and settled down to watch the proceedings from a safe distance. PC Yarwood, who had been knocked over by the crowd, staggered to his feet to find himself confronting a wild-eyed Larkin, who aimed his pistol at him. Knocking the gun upwards, Yarwood felt the bullet whiz past his head and unhurt, dashed off in the direction of Belle Vue Prison. Spying a cab not far from the bridge, he hailed it and shouted to the driver to go with all speed.

The enterprise now almost descended into farce as it was realised that someone had forgotten to bring the tools needed to force open the rear door of the van. Condon was eventually given the blame for this, but many years later, in his memoirs, he insisted that he had been planning the raid entirely on his own and that he could not be responsible for every single thing.

Meanwhile, amongst the mass of Irishmen struggling around the arches, the most prominent of the rescuers was seen to be William O'Meara Allen, a twenty-year-old

The attack on the van, from a contemporary print. (Author's collection)

Modern-day version of the bridge where the ambush took place. The van was stopped on the left-hand side of the picture. (© A. Hayhurst)

Irishman living along Rochdale Road, an out of work joiner. He carried a pair of pistols which he waved wildly, exhorting his fellow rescuers to greater efforts and menacing the crowd if they got too near. It was Allen who had shot the unfortunate Sprosson in the foot.

Inside the van, there was chaos. Sergeant Brett was trying to keep his charges cool, although in this he was badly hampered by the three women, who had been allowed to stand in the corridor with him. The noise inside the van was fearful, with repeated attacks of the roof and door and several voices outside shouting to him to hand out the keys, so that the rear door could be opened. This Brett stoutly refused to do, 'I must do my duty,' he muttered to himself as he tried to look through the grill in the rear door, which someone was just then attempting to jam open with a stone. One of the women prisoners, Emma Halliday, caught hold of Brett by his sleeve. 'Oh, come away, Charlie. You'll get shot,' she entreated, but Brett shook her away. Suddenly, the barrel of a pistol was poked through the open grill and a shot rang out. Brett immediately slumped to the floor. 'Charlie's killed,' screamed one of the women and there was a renewed demand from outside for the keys to be passed out. One of the women frantically felt in Brett's pockets and, discovering a ring with three keys on it, threw it through the grill and in less than a minute, the rear door had been flung open and the women were roughly pushed aside, Brett's body falling out on to the road. 'Kelly? Deasy?' the words were heard dimly through the racket, 'Here,' came the reply and after some fumbling with the keys, both men were released, although still manacled at the wrists. Despite their cries, none of the other prisoners were set loose and as the men came out of the van, Allen was heard to shout to Kelly, 'Didn't I say I'd die for you before I'd give you up.'

The main body of attackers now began to quit the scene, leaving the three women prisoners alone with the body of Sergeant Brett, now huddled on the roadside. Reinforcements were beginning to arrive from Belle Vue and a few Irishmen remained by the side of the road, waving pistols to deter anyone from following the main body as they streamed away across the fields. Kelly and Deasy were amongst the first of them and were soon spirited away, but prison warders gradually began to take a hold of the proceedings and lay hands on the other escaping men. Still to be seen, running towards the brickfields at an ever slowing pace, was Michael Larkin. He had recently been ill and after his violent exertions in the rescue, was now beginning to feel the pace. His companions, Allen and O'Brien, slowed down to help their comrade, but the three men were overtaken and badly beaten by the following crowd. Elsewhere in the rough and tumble, Condon himself was also badly handled by the mob and overpowered. At the police station, he was found to be in possession of a pistol and a sum of money totalling over £8. The unfortunate Sergeant Brett was taken to the hospital, where he died the following morning, a bullet having pieced his head, removing an eye from its socket.

Sergeant Charles Brett. (Courtesy of Alan and Marie Elmer)

Charles Brett's grave in Harpurhey Cemetery. (© A. Hayhurst)

A reward of £200 was offered by the magistrates for the arrest of any of the conspirators and a further £300 was added for the capture of Kelly and Deasy. Kelly was described as being thirty-five years old, 5ft 6in high, with hazel eyes, brown hair and weighing about eleven stone five pounds. His fellow conspirator, Deasy, was said to be twenty-nine years old, with hazel eyes and dark brown hair, and had a scar on his left cheek.

In Fenian Circles, expressions of unbridled joy were soon evident, both in England and Ireland, where the news quickly circulated, but this joy was soon tempered by the number of Irishmen who were being arrested. It was now dangerous to be Irish in Manchester and even more so if the accent was Irish-American. Altogether, over forty men were arrested and locked up in the next few days, including Allen, Larkin, and William Gould (a false name given by O'Brien), Condon (calling himself Edward Shore) and a man named Thomas Maguire, a Royal Marine, on leave from his regiment.

The issue of the *Manchester City News* of 28 September 1867 carried an account of the funeral of Sergeant Brett, with crowds of up to 30,000 said to have lined the route. Prominent amongst the mourners were: the Lord Mayor of Manchester and several members of the Corporation; Captain Palin, the Chief Constable; representatives of the Fire Brigade; a detachment of Salford police and the Manchester Police Band,

Plaque commemorating the attack, by the side of the modern-day bridge. (© A. Hayhurst)

behind which marched representatives of the four police divisions. Next came the hearse, with the pall being carried by six sergeants, followed by five coaches of mourners, including Brett's widow, his father, one brother and three daughters. The rear of the procession included twenty carriages of people who simply wished to show their respect for the deceased. Every available spot along the journey was occupied and on reaching the Harpurhey cemetery (where also lay the four Taylor children in their unmarked graves), the police formed a double line through which the cortège passed. The burial service was read by Revd Stamford Harris and at the conclusion of the service the police band played 'Luther's Hymn,' after which the mourners left.

The story of the brave sergeant had received a lot of publicity and sums of money were donated to Mrs Brett from all over the country. The Liverpool Police collected £32 and the sum of £100 was handed to the Chief Constable by Brett's colleagues, for the widow. The Manchester Watch Committee voted her the sum of 7s 6d per week for life.

On Thursday 26 September the hearing began before the City Magistrates. Forty-one people had so far been arrested on suspicion, but only twenty-nine were present in court, presided over by the Stipendiary Magistrate, Mr Robinson Fowler, together with the Mayor, Mr R. Neill, and no fewer than twenty Aldermen of the City. The court was defended by a strong body of the 8th Hussars, under Captain Briggs and a detachment of the 57th Foot, whilst the surrounding streets were protected by a cordon of police officers, some of whom were seen to be armed.

The dock was crowded as the manacled prisoners answered to their names. William O'Meara Allen, Henry Wilson, 'William Gould,' and 'Edward Shore' were defended by Mr Ernest Jones, and Michael Larkin, John Brennan, Patrick Kelly (Galway), John Bacon, William and John Martin were defended by Mr Cottingham. Michael Kennedy, Michael and Thomas Maguire, John Gleeson, Michael Morris, Michael and Thomas Ryan, Michael Corcoran, John Francis Nugent, James Sherry, Patrick Daly, Michael Joseph Boyland, Robert McWilliams, John Carrol, Charles Moorhouse, Patrick Kelly (Leitrim) Hugh Foley and Thomas Scalley were also before the court and the prosecution was conducted by Mr Higgin, Deputy Recorder for Manchester.

Mr Ernest Jones called the attention of the court to the fact that several of the prisoners, including the ones he was defending, were manacled at the wrists and he requested that orders be given for these to be removed immediately. Mr Cottingham also intervened, insisting that there were sufficient men to guard the prisoners in court and there was no reason, therefore, why the manacles should not be removed. There then followed a dialogue between Mr Fowler and the two lawyers, Fowler insisted that the matter of handcuffs had nothing to do with him and was the sole prerogative of the police. Accordingly, he declined to interfere.

Mr Higgins then began the prosecution, telling the court that he had been instructed by the Manchester authorities to prefer a charge against all the men now in custody, the charge being wilful murder. He went on to say that if any of

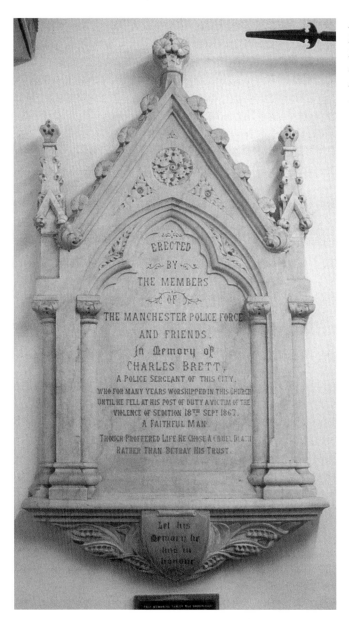

A plaque in the Tower Room of St Anne's Church, Mancester, originally in St Barnabas' Church, Ancoats, which closed in 1959. (© A. Hayhurst)

the prisoners could prove they were not at the scene of the crime, or being there did not take any part in the outrage, he would be glad to know it. He then described the events on the Hyde Road and told the court that of one thing there could be no doubt, Sergeant Brett had been murdered and that under the law of the land, all those involved would be equally guilty of murder. There was then a short break after which Ernest Jones again approached the matter of the manacles, claiming particularly that the wrists of Allen and Gould were badly swollen and Larkin was also complaining of extreme pain caused by the tight handcuffs. Once again,

Mr Fowler stoutly asserted that it had nothing to do with him and that it was entirely the business of the police whether the accused were manacled or not.

Announcing, 'I decline to sit in any court where the police over-ride the magistrates and will not lend myself to any such violation of the ordinary course of justice,' Ernest Jones swept out of the court, dramatically handing his brief to his instructing solicitor. Fowler thereupon turned to the four men now deprived of a defender and offered to suspend the hearing until further legal assistance could be obtained. The four men all insisted that if Mr Jones could not be their defender, they would have no other. All except Gould said that they would cross-examine witnesses themselves, but Gould insisted, 'If it is going to be a farce, I'll have nothing at all to do with it.' Finally, Fowler agreed that the handcuffs could be adjusted, where necessary, so that the prisoners were more comfortable and the hearing continued.

Witness Thomas Paterson, a puddler by trade, identified Allen as the man who had been on top of the van, trying to smash in the roof. He said that he had seen him, armed with two pistols, waving them at anyone who stood in his way and that he had put the pistols through the ventilator grill at the rear of the van, after which he heard a report and a scream from inside the van. Later, he saw Larkin, Allen and Gould making their way from the scene, with Allen again firing his revolvers and threatening to kill anyone who should come near. At the end of Paterson's evidence, Allen, Gould, Larkin and Wilson were asked if they wished to cross-examine, all declined.

George Pickup, a brickmaker, was next to give evidence. He had been in the vicinity of the Hyde Road bridge for most of the day and had seen the crowd of Irishmen and women gradually increase. When the prison van arrived, he saw a man wearing a white slop coat and greasy trousers firing a revolver at the policemen who were standing at the back of the van. Then a man wearing a light suit climbed on top of the van and tried to break through the roof, using a large stone which had been handed to him by someone below. Another of the party, who he identified as Larkin, tried to break open the rear door with a large hammer. Pickup then claimed that Allen, who he also identified, had shot at him twice and had also put his pistol through the ventilator and fired it. Allen had then wounded Sprosson and had fired another three or four shots through the ventilator of the van. After the rear door had been opened, it was Allen who entered the van and released Kelly and Deasy. He then saw the men run off across the fields and followed them, only to be threatened again by Allen's pistols. After some further discussion between defence counsel Mr Roberts, the prosecutor Mr Higgin and Mr Fowler, the magistrate agreed that one of the accused, John Gleeson, could stand down for lack of evidence and the court adjourned till the next day.

John Griffiths, a hairdresser with a shop on the Hyde Road, was the next witness and his evidence was largely on the lines of that given by Pickup. He singled out Allen as a man who had fired several shots. He also named Thomas Maguire, but said that he did not see Maguire do anything. Later, at the police station, he again identified Maguire and also Francis Nugent.

A young lad, twelve-year-old George Mulholland, claimed to have seen Allen firing at the horses and had heard him shouting at the driver, 'Stop, or I'll blow your brains out!' Later, he had seen Maguire on the roof of the van with a large stone, which had been handed to him by Larkin. At that stage, Larkin, plainly puzzled, called out, 'How do you know my name so well?' The prosecutor waved a hand at Larkin, 'Wait a minute and we'll see.'

Mulholland continued:

> I saw Larkin fire through the ventilator and I saw Allen take a hammer from a man and begin breaking in the door himself. One side of the hammer was shaped like a hatchet and he had a revolver in his other hand. I then saw Allen break the ventilator and Sergeant Brett had his hand up to prevent it being opened. Allen put the revolver to the ventilator and fired and I heard a woman's voice crying out immediately, 'He's killed.' I saw the man Sprosson shot in the foot. I think it was Larkin that did it.

Cross-examined by Mr Cottingham, Mulholland explained that he knew the names of these men as he had heard them calling to one another during the fracas; altogether amazing evidence from one so young.

Larkin, Allen, Thomas Maguire and, after some prompting, Gould, John Martin and Wilson were identified by John Beck, a railway clerk. The court then adjourned for refreshments, after which PC William Trueman, who was in the cab following on behind the van, entered the witness box. When the disturbance started, he had got down from the cab and ran towards the van, finding a crowd of about thirty men, half of whom appeared to be armed with pistols. He identified William Allen, who, he said, fired a pistol at him and he later saw Allen fire the pistol through the ventilator grill and heard a voice scream, 'He's shot.' Later, he accompanied the injured Sergeant Brett to the infirmary.

Several other witnesses identified a number of the participants in the attack, including Allen, Larkin, Gould and Thomas Maguire. This finished the business for the day apart from several men being called before the magistrates and released without charge for lack of evidence. On resumption next day, Mr Roberts told the court that several of the prisoners thought they were being identified by their positions in the dock and that witnesses were being tutored as to which was which. They therefore requested that they be allowed to change places and this request was agreed, the prisoners shuffling round into a different order. Then the first of the three women appeared to give evidence.

Eighteen-year-old Emma Hamilton described the scene in the van, with a hole being pounded in the roof by a large stone, which eventually dropped through and another stone being used to jam the ventilator open. Brett was asked several times by the men outside to give up the keys, but apart from muttering, 'God, it's them Fenians,' he stoutly refused to comply. 'I'll stick to my duty to the last,' he shouted and just then, she saw a pistol thrust through the ventilator. She caught hold of Brett's arm, saying, 'Oh, Charlie, Do come away,' and as she pulled the sergeant back, his

*Monument to the martyrs
in Moston Cemetery, from
a contemporary photograph.
(Author's collection)*

head came on a level with the pistol. There was a loud noise and Brett fell to the floor. When asked if she could identify the man who fired the pistol, she looked at the dock and pointed to William Allen. Continuing, she said that Allen had repeatedly asked for Brett's keys to be handed out and on several occasions, the women claimed that they were too frightened to obey, whereupon Allen shouted, 'I'll blow your brains out if you don't give them up.' One of the women eventually got the keys from the injured policeman's pocket and handed them through the ventilator. In a short time, the rear door was opened and breaking free, Hamilton then ran as fast as she could go to Belle Vue Prison.

The monument as it is today. (© A. Hayhurst)

A detail of the martyrs' monument. (© A. Hayhurst)

Ellen Cooper was next. She had little to add apart from the fact that Sergeant Brett was grimly holding on to the ventilator in a vain attempt to keep it shut. She, too, identified Allen as the man who fired the fatal shot, as did the next witness, twelve-year-old Joseph Partington, who was locked in a cell with another prisoner, under committal to the Industrial School at Ardwick. From his position in the van, he saw a pale-faced man wearing a blue tie come into the van and shout for Kelly. This man was identified as Allen. The third woman, Frances Armstrong, said that once the door was opened, it was Allen who pulled her out of the van, during which she tripped over Brett's body.

Further evidence was given relating to the capture of Larkin, who was being roundly assaulted until a warder from the Gaol, Joseph Howard, came up and told the crowd to desist. An elderly PC Knox, one of the officers in charge of the van, described how he faced up to a man waving a gun and after telling him, 'Man, do not be foolish,' struck a pose, stamped his foot firmly on the ground and smote his breast, saying, 'Fire then, you cowardly rascals and be damned to you.' This brought laughter in court.

At the end of the day's proceedings, more accused men were released for lack of evidence and as the hearing went on, it was becoming ever clearer that the police had made indiscriminate arrests and that anyone they could find with an Irish accent had been roped in.

On Monday, the fourth day of the hearing, it was noticeable that many of the accused were now no longer wearing manacles. Mr Roberts again asked the magistrates to order the remaining handcuffs to be taken off, which Mr Fowler again refused and a succession of witnesses then gave evidence. Elizabeth Robinson, a bystander and James Mayer, a barman, identified Allen, Gould and several more. Henry Wilson Black, the proprietor of an omnibus which had followed the cab behind the van, singled out Maguire whilst his driver, Josiah Munn, identified Allen, Larkin, Maguire, Nugent and John Martin.

Charles Pullitt, who had been driving the prison van, described a large piece of paving stone, weighing nearly 70lbs, which he found on the front step of the van when it reached the gaol. Other witnesses followed, each attesting to the presence of one or more of the conspirators at the scene.

Mr J.R. Woodcock, house surgeon at the Royal Infirmary said that Sergeant Brett had died from a wound in the head, the bullet entering the right orbit and passing out on the right side of the crown of the head. Sprosson had been admitted to hospital at the same time, as had PC Bromley, who had received a bad wound in the thigh and whose life was still in danger. At this stage, Mr Higgin withdrew the name of Patrick Kelly (Leitrim) from the list of accused and he was allowed to leave the dock. The hearing rose shortly afterwards and resumed the next morning and again a string of witnesses identified one or more of the accused.

The evidence of PC Charles Schofield, who identified William Martin, Allen and Nugent, was questioned because he had been in the court on the previous day carrying out his police duties. 'Then you should not have been!' snorted Fowler,

A copy of a contemporary 'Martyr's poster'. (Author's collection)

These are the three young Heroes, who for their country died,
They shall be long remembered by every Erin's child.
They lost their lives in a noble cause by English treachery,
They lost their lives for Ireland's sake, their native Country.

LARKIN   ALLEN   O'BRIEN

THE MARTYRS OF IRELAND

In all that fought for Ireland, they were the noblest ever seen,
They fought to gain a victory, all for the Emerald Green.
This victory once accomplished, will give us our native land,
T'will remind of us our Martyrs, who fought for Ireland.
M' P.D. Farrell

before allowing the examination to continue. Further witnesses gave their evidence and then Michael Corcoran and Hugh Foley were released for lack of evidence. The evidence for the prosecution was thus concluded and the prisoners were remanded until the following day, when the defence case began.

Mr Cottingham pointed out that the evidence against some of the men was trivial in the extreme and that witnesses were claiming to have identified named individuals out of a crowd of fifty or sixty people. One man had been identified by only two witnesses, one of whom was at least 30yds away. 'Was that sufficient proof on such a serious charge?' he pleaded.

Mr Bennett then addressed the court on behalf of Kennedy, Maguire and Ryan, calling particular attention to that evidence which he considered unreliable or doubtful. He was followed by Mr Roberts on behalf of his clients. He said that there were many spectators to the incident who took no part in it and who had no sympathy with it, or its cause. 'On the other hand,' he said, 'there were probably many people who had taken part in the attack who were not in court today.'

After the opening speeches of the various defence lawyers, the defence witnesses were called. Several attested that they had seen John Brennan two or three times on the day of the attack and that he had been nowhere near the Hyde Road bridge. He was backed up by Mary Bird, who said that she had seen Brennan at quarter to four and again ten minutes later in Oak Street, Shudehill.

Two witnesses appeared for Patrick Kelly (Galway) and told the court that Kelly was bagging potatoes with them at the time the van was being attacked. On the eighth day of the hearing, further witnesses were called, including those for Maguire, one of whom claimed to have seen him every half hour on the afternoon of the 18th. Other witnesses claimed to have seen Michael Maguire and Nugent at various times during the day, well away from the scene of the attack.

Elizabeth Perkins, a widow, said that Thomas Maguire lodged with her and had been in bed up until 3 p.m. on the 18th and had remained in her house until seven o'clock. Her next-door neighbour, Mary Ingham, also spoke in favour of Maguire and said she had seen him washing himself in the yard at about quarter past four. The hearing was then adjourned until the morrow, when after more defence witnesses had been heard, the twenty-three men remaining in the dock were formally committed to stand trial at the next Assizes on a charge of wilful murder. In the meantime, there was absolutely no news of Kelly and Deasy, who, despite occasional rumours of sightings, had completely disappeared.

It was decided that a Special Commission should be appointed to hear the case against the accused Fenians and Mr Justice Blackburn and Mr Justice Mellor arrived in Manchester to conduct it, with the Attorney General, Sir John Kerslake, appearing for the prosecution. It was announced that special arrangements had been made for the safety of the jury during the case, which was expected to last several days and the prisoners were escorted daily to and from the New Bailey Prison by a squadron of the 8th Hussars and two companies of the 72nd Foot (the Seaforth Highlanders). The court and the surrounding streets were protected by armed constables and a huge crowd lined the streets to see the arrival of the large van belonging to Salford Borough police, drawn by four horses, bearing the accused.

A Grand Jury of twenty-three notables was sworn in, with Sir Robert Tolver Garrard, Bart of Bryan as their foreman. Others included the Hon. A.F. Egerton MP, Sir William Henry Fielden, and Sir Gilbert Greenall MP. The number of men now charged was twenty-six and included William O'Meara Allen, William Gould, Edward Shore, Michael Larkin, Thomas Maguire, John Francis Nugent, William Martin, Michael Joseph Boyland, and John Carroll.

Mr Justice Blackburn opened the proceedings by saying that this trial would be by Special Commission and would concern itself with the outrages committed within the City of Manchester. He outlined the basic facts of the attack on the van, 'But,' he told the jury, 'the principal crime they would have to consider would be the murder of Sergeant Charles Brett.' He also made clear that although there was evidence that the prisoner Allen fired the fatal shot, everyone who aided and abetted him was equally guilty of murder.

After further instruction from the judge, the Grand Jury retired and returned at noon with a true bill against Allen, Gould, Larkin, Shore and Thomas Maguire for murder. These five men were then placed in the dock and all five pleaded 'Not Guilty' to the charge. Mr Digby Seymour announced that he was appearing for Allen, Shore and Gould, along with Mr Ernest Jones. Sergeant O'Brien, along with Mr Cottingham, were for Larkin and Maguire, and shortly afterwards, the court adjourned for the day.

The trial proper commenced at nine o'clock on Tuesday 29 October, when Digby Seymour QC applied for the trial to be removed to the Central Criminal Court (Old Bailey) in London. Mr Justice Blackburn, somewhat taken aback by this request, insisted that the request was 'Perfectly impossible.' The names of the jury were then drawn by ballot and the selection was completed with only one man, Benjamin Wortham, from the City of Manchester itself. The remainder were from Castleton near Rochdale, Bolton, Ashton-under-Lyne and Bury.

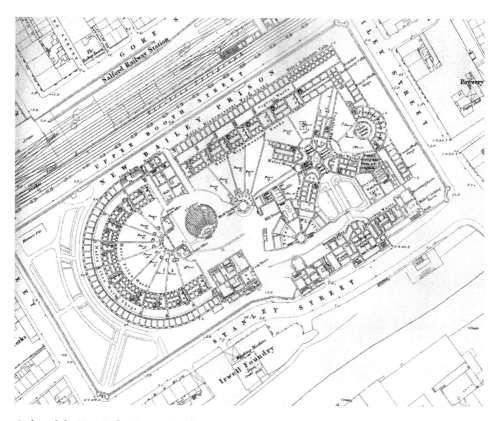

A plan of the New Bailey Prison. (Author's collection)

Opening the case, the Attorney General outlined the actions that had taken place on the Hyde Road once the police van had arrived at the railway arch. He gave a graphic description of the attack on the van, the demands being made for Brett to hand out the keys and him stoutly refusing, then the firing of the fatal shot through the ventilator in the rear door. He went on to describe the eventual handing out of the keys and the final release of Kelly and Deasy and their escape across the brickfields on to the Ashton Road. He told the court:

> I believe that you will find beyond all doubt that although it was Allen that fired the shot that killed Brett, all the other prisoners who are present today were present and active on that occasion, using their revolvers, Allen using two in forcing back the crowd, firing at the door and through it. The parts taken by the different prisoners will be described by the witnesses and you will find that each of them was active in the desperate affair which took place and which resulted in the death of Charles Brett.

Then came a long parade of witnesses to describing what they had heard and seen and as at the magistrates hearing, variously identified all of the men who stood in the dock before them, mostly using their names. PC Seth Bromley, now much improved in health, told how he had confronted Allen, who pointed his pistol directly at him and shot him in the thick of the thigh. PC Trueman then described how Gould fired at him and only just missed as he ducked down. It must have been clear to the court as witness followed witness that William Allen had taken a major part in the attack and had fired his pistols indiscriminately at whoever got in his way. Another witness, William Batty, identified Larkin and Shore, who was handing up a large stone to the man on the roof of the van and the hearing then adjourned for the night. The following day, a succession of witnesses told their stories, each one identifying one or more of the five accused and William Hughes, an engine fitter, said he saw Allen on top of the van, with Maguire handing stones up to him. After the prisoners in the van escaped, he saw Allen run at the crowd and fire.

Eventually, it was the turn of the defence witnesses, the first being Mary Flanagan, who said that she had seen Gould on the afternoon of 18 September as she walked past a pub near the city gaol at Belle Vue at about ten minutes to four. What evidence she could give was largely negated when she had to admit, under cross-examination, that she was presently lodging with a Mrs Wilson, whose husband was one of the men currently awaiting trial.

Isabella Fee, a beerhouse keeper in Rochdale Road, thought she might have seen Shore in her establishment at quarter to four on the 18th, but could not swear definitely that it was him. It was then the turn of Elizabeth Perkins, a widow who said she was the sister of Thomas Maguire. He lodged with her whenever he came home from the Marines and she remembered him being arrested at about midnight on the 18th at a neighbour's house. During that day, he had got up at about half past three in the afternoon, after complaining of feeling ill and he did not leave the house until about ten to seven that evening. The fact that he was in the house at three thirty was also confirmed by several other witnesses. PC Bean said that he knew Maguire well and that he was a quiet man and although he drunk a lot, it was usually at home.

The fifth day of the trial began and Mr Seymour addressed the jury on behalf of Allen, Gould and Shore. 'With regard to the witness Flanagan, either she committed perjury,' he said, 'or her evidence freed Gould of any complicity in the attack on the van, for if she had seen him at ten to four by the prison, he could not have been by the bridge when the shots were fired.' Much of the rest of his speech, which went on for over three hours, dealt with possibilities, rather than hard facts, for the small number of witnesses for the defence had given him little on which to base a plea for an acquittal. Sergeant O'Brien reviewed the evidence for Larkin and Maguire and spoke for a far shorter time than Digby Seymour, for he too was hampered by the lack of evidence favourable to his clients.

Mr Justice Blackburn then summed up, emphasising that murder amounted to killing a person without legal excuse or justification. It did not need there to be an intent to kill a particular person to make it murder. If a number of persons agreed to do a certain act and for the purpose of carrying out that act it was part of their intention to use dangerous violence, they were all guilty of the result of that violence. He added that the jury would have little difficulty in finding that those taking part had an intention to use dangerous violence and in conclusion, he called upon the jury to give their verdict fearlessly according to the evidence. The jury then retired and only just over an hour later, returned with a verdict of 'Guilty' against all five of the accused.

The five men were now asked if they had anything to say and Allen was first to be heard. He said first that he wished to review the evidence, but was hastily told by Mr Justice Blackburn that it was too late for that. Allen then continued that he was as innocent of the charge as any man in the courtroom. '[Allen] did not say that for the sake of mercy,' he said. '[Allen] would have no mercy. He would die in defence of his country.' Finally, he announced that his name was not William O'Meara Allen, but William Philip Allen, from County Cork. 'Justice had not been done to him,' he said, but concluded by thanking Mr Roberts for his advocacy.

Larkin then addressed the court, saying that he very much regretted the death of Sergeant Brett and that as to having a pistol, he had never used a revolver or a pistol that would have taken the life of a child, let alone a man. He had been there for the purpose of freeing 'Those two heroes,' Kelly and Deasy and admitted that he had had a fair trial, but he considered that some of the witnesses had sworn his life away. He hoped that God would forgive them.

Gould came next and made a long speech on the wrongs done to Ireland, during which he announced that his real name was Captain Michael O'Brien, born in the County of Cork and lately of the US Army on the Federal side.

Thomas Maguire repudiated all connections with Fenianism and strongly protested his innocence, being in bed at the time of the attack, as several witnesses had testified.

Shore followed, telling the court that his real name was Edward O'Meagher Condon and he, too, claimed his innocence and said that if he had not been an Irishman, he would never have been arrested. His final words were, 'God Save Ireland,' which was repeated by the other four.

Mr Justice Mellor then pronounced sentence of death and told the condemned men that they had been severally convicted of the crime of wilful murder, after a full, patient and impartial investigation. 'If I were to hold out any hope of a pardon, I would be misleading you,' he said. The prisoners then shook hands with their counsel and were taken down. As they disappeared, Maguire shouted out again, 'God Save Ireland!' The next day, the remaining accused men were found 'Not Guilty' of murder. It seemed that for justice to be seen to be done, the lives of just five Irishmen were to be enough.

However, there was much agitation about the position of Thomas Maguire and a petition was raised by twenty-two members of the press, addressed to the Secretary of State for the Home Department, stating that they conscientiously believed that Maguire was innocent of the crime for which he had been convicted. A letter from the Home Office dated 12 November 1867 confirmed that there was good reason to believe that Maguire's defence was true and an unconditional pardon was granted. Maguire, who had meantime been dismissed from the Marines for murder, was subsequently reinstated.

Strenuous efforts continued to be made on behalf of the remaining four prisoners, with public meetings being held up and down the country, although not all were in favour of the condemned men. Catholics attending mass at Salford Cathedral were recommended to keep away from the executions, which were due to be held in public at the New Bailey Prison and just a few days before the execution date, a letter from the Home Office reached the New Bailey, advising that the sentence on Condon had been reduced to penal servitude for life. Condon was an American citizen and pressure had been put on the British Government by the Americans, resulting in the lesser sentence. Condon served eleven years and then went back to the USA.

There were now just three condemned men in the New Bailey and their spiritual needs were looked after by Father Gadd, a young curate at St John's Cathedral, who was actually on holiday in Ireland when he received an urgent message, asking him to return home immediately to look after the condemned men. This he did, hastening to the prison to look after the men he always described as 'My boys'. The three men had been placed in condemned cells all adjoining and Gadd would kneel in the corridor offering up prayers, whilst his charges repeated the responses. 'How they prayed,' Gadd said later. 'I never had more devotional penitents in my life.' On the day before the execution, he arranged for Canon Cantwell of St Patrick's Church to attend to William Allen and Father Quick from St Wilfrid's parish to do the same for Larkin, telling them that he would take care of O'Brien himself.

The morning of Saturday 23 November dawned dark and miserable. A huge crowd had assembled throughout the night to gaze on the scaffold, which was protruding through the upper section of the New Bailey Prison wall. An appeal to the Home

Secretary for a reprieve having failed, preparations went ahead and the executioner William Calcraft arrived at the prison. Larkin and Allen were allowed final visits from their relatives (O'Brien had no close relatives in England) and the three men were awakened at quarter to five on the appointed day from what Gadd said were 'Tranquil and profound slumbers'. It is not likely that this was actually the case as Larkin, in particular, was in a very distressed state. The three men received Mass and Holy Communion and then at quarter to eight, the solemn procession led by Calcraft and his assistant Armstrong, the prison officials, the three priests and their charges made their way onto the scaffold, which was draped in black cloth so that, when the trap fell, nothing would be seen of the executed men as they hung there for the statutory hour. All three men left final letters in which they again protested their innocence, O'Brien claiming to the last that he was not present when the van was attacked.

When the drop fell, Allen died instantly, but it was soon obvious that Larkin and O'Brien were still very much alive. The drop had been too short, a not infrequent happening at executions in those days and Calcraft hurried below the scaffold where, to Gadd's horror, he hung his full weight around Larkin's legs to finish him off in the time honoured way. (The other two priests had left the scaffold as soon as the trap fell). Satisfied that Larkin was now dead, he turned his attention to O'Brien, only to

Father Gadd, who administered the Last Rites to the condemned men. (Author's collection)

be forced away by Father Gadd, who forbade the hangman to touch him. Gadd then stood in front of the suspended man, offering a crucifix to his twitching fingers and there he stood for three quarters of an hour until O'Brien breathed his last. Whether this did O'Brien any favours is a moot point, but the horror-stricken catholic priest did his best under appalling circumstances and no blame can be attached to him. Later, he presided over the burial of the three in the prison grounds.

In 1871, the prison was taken down to make way for the extension to Salford station and the bodies were reburied at Strangeways Prison, where their graves are now marked solely by mysterious marks on the wall. In 1877, an impressive memorial to the 'Manchester Martyrs' was erected at the Catholic Moston Cemetery, (paid for by the Irish people) and the foundation stone was dedicated by James Stephens, who came specially from Ireland. The effigies of Allen, Larkin and O'Brien look down from the middle of the memorial, just below a large Celtic cross and for many years, on the anniversary of the executions, a procession walked through the city to the memorial, after which a service followed. Events in Ireland, plus agitation from the National Front, led to this ceremony being discontinued during the 1970s. Timothy Deasy died in America in 1880 whilst Kelly lived on until 1908. James Stephens, having spent twenty years as an exile in France, died in Dublin in 1901.

St Patrick's Church, Livesey Street,
where Michael O'Brien's last letter to his
brother, written in the goal, is preserved.
(© A. Hayhurst)

3

'FOR THAT I DON...'

Seymour Grove, Manchester, 1879

Charles Frederick Peace was born on 14 May, 1832, in Angel Court, Nursery Street, Sheffield. His father, John Peace, had been a miner, but lost a leg in an industrial accident and had perforce to give up mining. Eventually, he built up a business as an animal trainer and whilst following this occupation, he met and married a Royal Naval surgeon's daughter, as a result of which, Charles (later known as 'Charlie') was born. His siblings were Mary Ann, the eldest, Dan and young Willie. Their home life was as comfortable as any working-class home could be in the industrial hell-hole that was Sheffield at the time and Charlie was sent out to work at the age of twelve, first apprenticed to a tinsmith and later in the steel trade.

There, he suffered a horrendous accident, when a bolt of white hot steel went clean through his leg, putting him in hospital for eighteen months, at the end of which time the doctors could do nothing more for him and he returned home. Lady Luck does not seem to have favoured young Charlie, as apart from a permanent limp, he also suffered damage to his face and lost a finger from his left hand; but despite these impediments, he mastered the art of violin playing and on occasions he gave impromptu concerts, often being billed as the 'Modern Day Paganini!'

As an adult, Charlie grew to the height of 5ft 4in with a shock of wiry brown hair and occasionally grew a beard. His jaw deformity enabled him to manipulate his face so that he could make himself unrecognisable, even to close friends and this came in handy, for when he left his work at the steel factory at the end of the day, he started work at his other occupation, that of a thief. This led on to burglary and for the next twenty years, Charlie Peace was the scourge of the North East, breaking into any house that took his fancy, often choosing to break in at bedroom level, first of all shinning up a drain pipe and then jemmying open a window. He would then wander through the house, often tip-toeing past the

Charles Peace, from a contemporary photograph. (Author's collection)

sleeping occupants, looking for jewellery or anything portable that would make money; piling everything together on one spot, so that when he was ready, he could gather it all up and shin down the drain pipe to make his getaway. However, he didn't always get clear away and between 1851 and 1858, Peace was in and out of prison, although he always returned to his old criminal ways as soon as he had the opportunity. In 1859, he also acquired a wife, Hannah Ward, although the author has been unable to discover a marriage registration.

Hannah was soon pregnant and this pregnancy was complicated by the fact that Charlie got six years for theft at Manchester Assizes and saw little of his wife and family until 1865, having done the full term of punishment. This time when he came out, he attempted to set up a legitimate business as a picture framer and indeed, was quite good at it, employing two men. Gradually, however, the longing to be back burgling came to the surface and within a few short months he was again at Manchester Assizes where this time, he got seven years under the name of George Parker. He served time in several prisons, being released in 1872 and returned to the long-suffering Hannah, who was now living in Orchard Street, Sheffield, keeping body and soul together by taking in washing.

During his latest spell in prison, Peace had thought long and hard about his criminal existence and the penalties incurred therein and he made a solemn vow to himself that this stretch would be his last. On regaining his freedom, he took to carrying a pistol and as events were to show, he would not hesitate to use it. He now presented himself to the world as a respectable artisan during the day, but in the darkness of the night, he launched into a veritable frenzy of burglaries, travelling all over the north of England, breaking in wherever the fancy took him. Now, he was making a considerable amount of money from his nocturnal activities and he took to wearing expensive clothes when he went out. His prison terms and the vow that he would not fall into police hands again sharpened his wits and he took to surveying the properties he wished to burgle, watching them carefully for a few days before making his move.

By 1875, he and his family (there were now two children) were living at 40 Victoria Place, Britannia Road, Darnall, a suburb of Sheffield, where one day by chance, he bumped into the local vicar, the Revd Littlewood. To Peace's horror, he recognised the vicar as the former Chaplain of Wakefield Prison, although Charlie did not at first realise that the vicar had not recognised him. He went to see Littlewood, who was somewhat surprised to see him but listened patiently whilst Peace poured out his story and begged the clergyman not to give him away. Having given the matter some thought, the clergyman agreed to keep Charlie's secret, on the strict understanding that from then on, Peace and his family would lead a respectable life and would become regular worshippers at his church. Peace had little option but to agree and until they moved out of the area, Charlie and Hannah and their two children Willie and Jane, attended church regularly and Peace even taught at the Sunday School. To all outward appearances, the Peace family were now truly respectable, but the vicar might not have been so confident about his successful reforming of an old lag if he had known that Charlie Peace had taken a fancy to his next-door-but-one neighbour, the twenty-five-year-old Mrs Catherine Dyson. Catherine, whilst good looking, was not really a beauty, but she was tall, with jet black hair. It is a strange fact that women are often attracted to ugly little men and before long, Catherine was responding to his advances and spending the occasional evening with Charlie in one of the local Music Halls. Peace's relationship with Catherine Dyson was not without its dangers, as her husband, Arthur Dyson, was 6ft 3in tall and built accordingly. He had been working in the USA as a railway engineer, but ill health had forced him to return home at the age of forty-eight.

However, Dyson was something of a gentle giant and although he suspected that something was going on between his wife and Charlie Peace, he made little or no attempt to stop it. At one time, in frustration, he wrote on a visiting card, 'Charles Peace is requested not to have anything to do with my family' and posted it through Charlie's door, but the little man took no notice and if anything, redoubled his attempts to gain Catherine's affections. Whilst it is certain that Catherine initially responded to Peace's approaches, she soon tired of him and warned him off, but this did not stop him lurking about in the street, peering through the Dyson's window and generally making a nuisance of himself. On occasion, he would follow Arthur Dyson as he went about his business, shouting obscenities, presumably feeling safe from retaliation because of Dyson's rather diffident nature.

Eventually, Mrs Dyson applied to the Magistrates Court for a restraining order against Peace, demanding that he cease to bother her and her husband. The cause of this was an incident when Mrs Dyson accosted Peace and demanded to know why he was causing so much trouble to her husband. Peace went into a paroxysm of rage and, drawing a pistol from his jacket, pointed it straight at Mrs Dyson and told her he would blow her brains out and her husband's too! Whether the news of this incident reached Charlie's wife is not known, but soon afterwards, the family moved to Hull, where she opened an eating-house.

Meanwhile, Charlie Peace kept on with his burglaries and on the evening of 1 August 1878, he was in the vicinity of Seymour Grove, Manchester, a respectable area with large houses, well suited to his method of operation. At about twenty minutes to midnight, a young law student, John Massey Simpson, was walking home when he met PC Nicholas Cock, on his beat. Cock had been in the police force for less than a year and was still somewhat wet behind the ears and the locals had affectionately nick-named him 'The Little Bobby'. Earlier that day, he had been in court, a witness in the prosecution of the Habron Brothers, three Irish navvies, on a charge of drunkenness. This was not the first time that the Habrons had been in court on similar charges and they were not best pleased to find themselves landed with a fine. One of the brothers, William, was so incensed that he shouted at Cock that he would shoot him. Nobody took this very seriously, except Cock, who complained to his Superintendent, only to have his complaint brushed off. 'The Habrons,' Superintendent Bent told the troubled constable, 'were good workers and only ever gave trouble when they were in drink.'

Simpson and PC Cock walked to where Seymour Grove, Upper Chorlton Road and Manchester Road met, forming a small grassy triangle, known as West Point. Nearby was an unoccupied house formerly owned by a Mr John Gratrix, and they saw the bulky figure of PC Beanland approaching them down Upper Chorlton Road. He joined the group and they chatted for several minutes, when Simpson noticed a shadowy figure at the entrance to Seymour Grove. As the man passed under the street lamp, Simpson saw that he was dressed in a short brown coat and wearing a pot hat. The stranger paused briefly to stare at the three men, before moving on into the darkness.

Minutes later, the little group broke up and went their separate ways, Cock going up Seymour Grove. Simpson had walked about 150yds in the opposite direction when he heard the sound of a shot, followed immediately by a second report. Running back in the direction of West Point, he heard someone shout, 'Murder, Murder! Oh, I'm shot!' and he then came upon PC Beanland, lustily blowing his police whistle. Apart from two men with night-soil wagons, there was nobody else in sight. Then they saw the crumpled body of PC Cock, lying on the pavement, and PC Beanland knelt down to cradle his colleague's head in his arms. Simpson unfastened the constable's tunic and found blood spurting from a wound in his chest. Cock was still conscious and Beanland asked, 'Who shot you?'

'Leave me alone and I'll tell you,' muttered the wounded policeman. Beanland asked again, 'Who shot you' and Cock, now obviously confused by his injury, replied, 'I don't know. You're killing me.' The two night-soil men now came running up and one of them helped to put Cock on his wagon and took him to the nearby surgery of Dr Dill, still alive, but obviously in a grave condition.

Whilst Dr Dill tried his best to stem the flow of blood, Superintendent Bent arrived, shortly after which Nicholas Cock died. Bent then appears to have made

Modern-day Seymour Grove, from West Point. (© A. Hayhurst)

a hasty decision. Remembering that Cock only that morning had complained that the Habron Brothers had threatened to shoot him, and perhaps feeling a little guilty at having laughed at the young constable's fears, he immediately decided that the brothers would have to be brought in. He was aware that the three Irishmen slept in an outhouse in a nursery belonging to a Mr Deakin, only a few hundred yards from West Point and after assembling reinforcements, he woke up Mr Deakin and explained his errand. He asked Deakin to approach the outhouse and knock on the door, asking for it to be opened, warning him that the Irishmen were probably armed and dangerous, but that as soon as the door opened, he would take over and go into the room first to make the arrest.

The undoubtedly brave Deakin approached the outhouse, knocking on the door and shaking it violently, three times. Muffled curses came from inside and Deakin ventured in a faltering voice 'Is Jack in?'

'Yes,' said someone and Deakin heard the sound of the lock being withdrawn. Hastily, he skipped out of the way as Bent and his policemen tumbled into the outhouse, which was in pitch darkness. By the light of their police lamps, they saw the three brothers, all stark naked, lying in bed. Bent rummaged amongst their discarded clothes to make quite sure that they contained no weapons and then brusquely commanded the brothers to get dressed and come with him to Old Trafford police station. 'Mind what I say to you,' he told the brothers, 'You three men are charged on suspicion of having killed and murdered PC Cock.' One of the brothers, John Habron, raised his handcuffed wrists. 'I was in bed all the time,' he said, but was taken with his brothers to the police station and locked up for the rest of the night.

The eagle-eyed Superintendent Bent had spotted a footprint on the road at the entrance to Firs Lane, a private road leading off from West Point and he now had the Habrons' boots gathered together and carefully compared them. One boot, belonging to eighteen-year-old William Habron, matched exactly, including nail marks and indentations in the sole. Returning to Old Trafford police station, he examined clothing taken from the brothers and in William Habron's waistcoat pocket, he discovered two percussion caps from a pistol. Questioning Habron about these, the young man at first denied all knowledge of them, but later offered the unlikely explanation that they might already have been in the waistcoat pocket when Mr Deakin, the nurseryman, gave it to him. William Habron was now fully in the frame for the murder of PC Cock and he was charged, alongside his brother John, with murder, his other brother Frank Habron being released for lack of evidence.

The trial opened in Manchester on 27 November, in front of Mr Justice Lindley. Frederick Willcox, a watchmaker, told the court that he had cleaned a watch belonging to John Habron about three months ago and when he was returning it, Frank Habron had told him of words he had had with the 'Little Bobby' on the previous evening. Evidently, PC Cock had threatened to summon him and he went on, 'If the 'Little Bobby' ever does anything to me or any of my brothers, By God I'll shoot him!'

Donald McLennan, an ironmonger, gave evidence that William Habron had recently been in the shop and had asked to see some cartridges. He did not appear to know what sort of gun he needed the cartridges for and eventually left the shop without buying anything. Under cross-examination, he was certain that the man was William Habron. Other witnesses followed, with largely similar stories and then it was the turn of Superintendent Bent.

He told the court of the footprint he had discovered on Firs Lane and how he had found that William Habron's boot left identical markings. He was also able to show that the Habrons had lied about their whereabouts on the night of the murder. They had all claimed to be in bed by 9 p.m., but the police found witnesses to say that the brothers had been seen drinking in local pubs until eleven. Bent also said that just before entering the outhouse to make the arrests, he had seen a small light inside, which had been hastily extinguished when Mr Deakin first knocked on the door. Produced in court was a small piece of candle which Bent said was the probable cause.

PC Nicholas Cock, from a contemporary print. (Author's collection)

Bent's evidence must have made a considerable impression on the jury and in just under three hours, they brought in a verdict of 'Guilty' on William Habron, with a strong recommendation to mercy in view of his young age, whilst his brother John was found 'Not Guilty.' The death sentence was pronounced on William and he was taken to Strangeways Prison to await his fate. Habron was lucky, for he was reprieved less than forty-eight hours before the execution was due to take place and given a term of imprisonment. In view of what happened later, one has to wonder whether Superintendent Bent's evidence was not largely the product of his imagination.

Peace, the actual killer, later said that he was in the courtroom to hear sentence of death passed on the hapless William Habron, although this might just have been another of Charlie's boasts. However, what is clear is that the next day, Peace was back in Sheffield, and resolved to continue his pestering of Catherine Dyson, who with her husband had moved house to Banner Cross, on the Eccleshall Road. That evening, Catherine went to the outside privy in the courtyard and when she came out, Charlie Peace was there, making threats and waving a pistol at her. Speak, or I fire,' he snarled. Catherine gave a shriek, which was heard all round the courtyard and by Arthur Dyson, who was sitting quietly reading, in his house.

For once, the worm turned. The gentle Dyson had finally had enough and he stormed out into the yard to confront Peace. With no hesitation at all, Peace fired three times at Dyson, and the big man slumped to the ground without a word. Peace wasted no time in leaving the scene – he was well aware that if Dyson died, he would be wanted for murder and if he was caught, there could only be one outcome.

Neighbours, who had been alerted by the sound of shots, carried Dyson into the house and Dr Harrison was summoned urgently, but there was nothing he could do for the unfortunate Dyson, who died shortly after he arrived. The only sound in the front parlour of the cottage was muffled sobs coming from Catherine, who was scarcely able to take in the events of the past two hours, so quickly had things happened. Next morning, the area was searched thoroughly by the police, but of Peace, there was no sign and soon posters were all over Sheffield, offering a reward of £100 for information leading to the arrest and conviction of Charles Peace.

Meanwhile, Peace travelled first back to Hull, then on to York, then Manchester and several other large towns, burgling as he went. Early the following year, he was in Nottingham, where he made the acquaintance of a woman called Susan Bailey, recently divorced and existing on the proceeds of sewing. Peace was immediately attracted to Mrs Bailey and the two of them were soon living together, but this did not prevent Charlie carrying on his nefarious activities and he would often be away for days on end. Susan Bailey suspected that during these absences, he was going back to his wife and children for short periods but did nothing about it.

After one of his absences, Peace announced that they were moving to London and that his wife and their child Willie would join them there! Susan does not seem to have raised any objection to this *ménage a trois*, nor, for that matter does Hannah. Perhaps both women realised that Peace was a good provider, thanks to his burglary proceeds, and they were better off sharing him, rather than living alone.

Eventually, they ended up at 5 East Terrace, Evelina Road, Peckham, a large, eight-roomed house in which Peace set up as an antique dealer, filling the property with elegant furniture which he would invite prospective clients to inspect. He was now going under the name of Thompson and announced that Susan was his wife. They were well dressed when they went out, though Peace was always careful to disguise himself in case he should come across someone from the North who knew him and he affected the appearance of an elderly man, although he was only in his middle forties. To the world at large, his real wife was a lodger, Mrs Ward (her maiden name) and for the next eighteen months, they all appear to have lived happily together, although the neighbours chattered amongst themselves that Mrs Thompson was partial to drink.

Just after midnight on 2 October 1878, Peace was breaking into a house in Blackheath, the residence of a Mr Burness, when he was spotted by a patrolling constable, PC Robinson. Calling two of his colleagues, Sergeant Brown and PC Girling, Robinson waited in the back garden, whilst the other two went round the front. Suddenly, the French windows opened and the constable saw someone creeping out. Robinson made to apprehend the man, who shouted, 'Get back or I'll shoot!' This did not deter the policeman and again he moved forward. Suddenly, shots rang out, despite which the plucky Robinson leapt forward once again and grabbed

The killing of Arthur Dyson from a contemporary print. (Courtesy of Evans-Skinner Crime Archive)

at the shadowy figure in front of him. There was another shot, which missed and then another, which hit Robinson in the arm. Desperately, he made another grab for his assailant and succeeded in hanging on until the other two policemen arrived. Peace was arrested and taken down to the police station after giving the name of John Ward. The police had to accept this name at face value, for Peace's real name and history were unknown in London at that time. The next day he was remanded for a week and in the meantime, news of the capture reached Evelina Road. Knowing that the police would not be far behind, Hannah and Willie, with Susan Bailie, decamped, taking as much of the household goods as they could handle, the rest being hastily sold.

Peace, still in the name of John Ward, was sentenced to a long prison term for the attempted murder of PC Robinson and might well have remained there for the rest of his life, had he not written a letter to a friend of his, Mr Brion, asking him to visit him in prison. The letter was signed 'John Ward' and Mr Brion, not knowing who this was, went to Newgate and after asking for Ward, was amazed to see that it was his friend and fellow inventor, John Thompson. The two of them had collaborated in a scheme to raise sunken ships by pumping air into their hulls, although they had not, to date, managed to get anyone interested in financing the scheme.

Brion soon put the police on the right track and a search of the house in Evelina Road disclosed ample evidence of Charlie's nocturnal burglings. Probably realising that the gravy train had come to a halt, Sue Bailey contacted the police and told them that the man they knew as John Ward was actually Charles Peace, wanted for murder in Sheffield. She also politely reminded the police of the little matter of the £100 reward.

On 22 January 1879, Peace was put on a train, accompanied by Chief Warder Cosgrove and Warder William Robertson, bound for Armley Gaol in Leeds, where he was to be tried for the murder of Arthur Dyson. The train had no corridors and so anyone in a compartment had perforce to stay there until the train reached a station. As the train moved towards Sheffield, Peace felt the call of nature. Nothing could be done except to open the carriage window and Peace stood

Peace's attempted escape from a train, from a contemporary print. (Courtesy of Evans-Skinner Crime Archive)

Headline news of the escape and capture.
(Courtesy of Sheffield Daily Telegraph*)*

THIRD EDITION.

SHEFFIELD DAILY TELEGRAPH,
WEDNESDAY MORNING, JAN. 22, 9.30 A.M.

ESCAPE
AND
CAPTURE
OF
PEACE.

DARING LEAP FROM THE TRAIN.

there, manacled at the wrists, doing what he had to do when suddenly, he went head first through the window of the moving train. Warder Robertson had taken the precaution of linking a pair of handcuffs to the manacles that Peace was wearing and he was holding the other half of the handcuffs when Peace made his move. Robertson made a grab for Charlie's leg and held Peace, kicking and struggling, upside down outside the carriage, whilst Cosgrove tugged grimly on the communication cord to stop the train.

Outside the compartment, Peace, still upside down, had managed to get his hands on the steps and was straining to get away from Robertson's grasp when his shoe, which Robertson was holding, came off and he fell on to the line. Robertson now joined Cosgrove in a further assault on the communication cord, which stubbornly failed to act and at length, they managed to attract the attention of a signal man as they passed his cabin, and he signalled for the train to stop. The two warders raced back up the line just in time to see Peace recovering consciousness and complaining bitterly about his treatment! Without further delay, the warders collared Peace and this time, made sure he was delivered safely to the gaol.

A letter written by the Chief Constable of Sheffield, now in the National Archives, reads, 'I am not much surprised at his making such a desperate effort to escape and from what I learn from persons who were in the train at the time, I think no blame is attached to the accompanying prison officers.'

Peace was tried at Leeds on 4 February 1879 and found guilty of the murder of Arthur Dyson and sentenced to death. A letter dated 28 January, written by C.E. Vincent, Director of the CID to the Prisons Department, Home Office, said:

> Information has been received by the police that efforts will be made by the relatives and friends of the convict Peace to prevent his being executed, should he be found guilty of murder, by conveying poison to him in order that he may commit suicide ... the prisoner has made arrangements with his friends that they will visit him and carry in their mouths poison wrapped in tinfoil, which is to be passed to him in the act of kissing.

Vincent finished his letter, 'I forward this information for what it is worth.'

On the morning of 25 February Peace woke early and retreated into the toilet from where the warders watching over him struggled to extricate him. 'What's the matter,' grunted Peace. 'Are you being hanged today or me?' His last breakfast consisted of bacon and egg and again, Peace could not resist complaining, 'This is bloody rotten bacon!'

Charlie Peace in court, from a contemporary print. (Courtesy of Evans-Skinner Crime Archive)

Peace on the scaffold. (Courtesy of Evans-Skinner Crime Archive)

Special orders were issued on the day of the execution that no prisoner was to be out of his cell except for kitchen work, from 7.30 a.m. to 8.30 a.m. and that no person was to be admitted to the prison until 10 a.m. The prison engineer was detailed to take up his position at the prison flagstaff at 7.45 a.m. and to keep a sharp lookout for the Governor's signal, at which time he was to hoist the black flag. Shortly before eight o'clock, hangman William Marwood entered the condemned cell and pinioned Peace, who made no resistance. The procession, consisting of the Under Sheriff and Governor, the Chaplain, Warder Fenwick, Peace, Principal Warder Boan, Executioner, and Chief Warder moved forward in to the courtyard, flinching as they met a bitterly cold morning, with snow falling. They were accompanied by another six warders, three on each side of the procession. Marwood was handling the execution on his own, as the Governor's request for a 'Trusty Assistant' had been refused by the Home Office.

Once on the scaffold, Marwood drew the white cap over Charlie's head and fixed the noose, when the condemned man barked out, 'Stop! I should like a drink. Have you a drink to give me?' Marwood's reply was to pull the lever and send Charlie Peace into eternity. Immediately after the inquest, the Chief Warder, with Principal Warder Boan and warders Fenwick, Moffitt and Fox placed the body in a coffin and buried it in a specially prepared grave without further ceremony, watched by the Under Sheriff and the Governor.

Susan Bailey later made an official application for the £100 reward, although it is not clear whether she received any of it. PC Cock was buried in St Clements

EXECUTION OF CHARLES PEACE.

Yorkshire (West Riding Division). To Wit. } Declaration of Sheriff and others.

WE, the undersigned, hereby declare that Judgment of Death was this day executed on *CHARLES PEACE*, in Her Majesty's Prison, at Leeds, in the County of York, in our presence.

Dated this 25th day of February, One Thousand Eight Hundred and Seventy-nine.

W. GRAY, *Under-Sheriff.*
C. A. KEENE, *Governor of Her Majesty's Prison, Leeds.*
OSMOND COOKSON, *Chaplain, Her Majesty's Prison, Leeds.*
WM. NICHOLSON PRICE, *Surgeon, Her Majesty's Prison, Leeds.*
CHAS. J. WRIGHT, *Deputy-Surgeon.*
BENNET G. BURLEIGH, (Central News.)
J. ATKINS, (Sheffield Independent.)
J. MOORE, (Press Association.)
JAMES D. SHAW, (Leeds Mercury.)

CERTIFICATE OF SURGEON.

I, WILLIAM NICHOLSON PRICE, the Surgeon of Her Majesty's Prison, at Leeds, in the County of York, hereby certify that I this day examined the body of Charles Peace, on whom Judgment of Death was this day executed in the same Prison, and that on that examination I found that the said Charles Peace was dead.

Dated this 25th day of February, One Thousand Eight Hundred and Seventy-nine.

WILLIAM NICHOLSON PRICE.

CORONER'S INQUISITION.

BOROUGH OF LEEDS, IN THE COUNTY OF YORK. } AN INQUISITION indented, taken for our Sovereign Lady the Queen, at Her Majesty's Prison, in the Borough of Leeds, the twenty-fifth day of February, in the forty-second year of the reign of our Sovereign Lady Victoria, by the Grace of God, of the United Kingdom of Great Britain and Ireland, Queen, Defender of the Faith, and in the year of our Lord One Thousand Eight Hundred and Seventy-nine, pursuant to the directions of the "Capital Punishment Amendment Act, 1868," before John Cooper Malcolm, Gentleman, Coroner of our said Lady the Queen, for the said Borough, and in whose jurisdiction the said Prison is situated, on view of the body of Charles Peace, then and there lying dead, upon the oaths of the several persons whose names are hereunder written and seals affixed, good and lawful men of the said Borough, duly chosen, and who being then and there duly sworn and charged to enquire for our said Lady the Queen, when, how, and by what means the said Charles Peace came to his death, do upon their oath say that the said Charles Peace, who was of the age of forty-seven years, was a prisoner in the Prison aforesaid, and that at the Assizes and General Gaol Delivery held at Leeds, in and for the West Riding Division of the said County of York, on the twenty-eighth day of January, One Thousand Eight Hundred and Seventy-nine, before the Right Honorable Sir William Baliol Brett, Knight, Lord Justice of Appeal, and the Honorable Sir Henry Charles Lopes, Knight, one of the Judges of the High Court of Justice, he the said Charles Peace, was capitally convicted of the crime of Wilful Murder, and thereupon received the judgment of the Court that he the said Charles Peace should be hanged by the neck until he should be dead; and that the said judgment of death was duly executed upon the said Charles Peace on the said twenty-fifth day of February, in the year aforesaid, within the walls of the said Prison, in which prison the said Charles Peace was confined at the time of his execution, and that he died by hanging. And the Jurors aforesaid further say, that the body of the said Charles Peace now here lying dead and upon whom this Inquisition is held is the identical body of the said Charles Peace, who was so convicted, sentenced, and executed as aforesaid. And the Jurors aforesaid further say, that the Inquest now here held on view of the body of the said Charles Peace is held within Twenty-Four hours after his execution.

In witness whereof, as well the said Coroner as the Jurors aforesaid, have to this Inquisition set their hands and seals, on the day, year, and at the place first above-mentioned.

JNO. C. MALCOLM		THOMAS READ	
JOSIAH WALKER		CHARLES STOTT	
JOSEPH COLLINS		THOMAS BOWERS	
THOMAS ARTHUR SOWRY		STEPHEN GREENWOOD	
SEPTIMUS WILSDEN		JAMES BRITTON	
THOMAS MOOR		JOHN WILLIAM ROBERTS	
GEORGE WARING			

S. Moxon, Printer, Queen's Court, Briggate, Leeds.

The Execution statement. (Crown copyright)

churchyard, Chorlton-cum-Hardy, but the grave became neglected and the headstone was later removed to the Police Headquarters at Preston. It reads:

To the memory of Nicholas Cock.

An able and energetic officer of the County Constabulary who on 2 August 1876 while engaged in the faithful discharge of his duty was cruelly assassinated. This monument was raised by voluntary contribution; the subscribers consisting of Magistrates, The Officers and Men of his own Force and citizens in general who felt that some public tribute was due to the name of one who, while in his private capacity deserved well of those who knew him, for zeal and fidelity in his office was worthy of honoured remembrance by all.

Aged 20 years.
Be thou faithful unto Death
And He will give thee a crown of life.

In the Black Museum at Scotland Yard there is a showcase containing Peace's pick-locks, jemmies and a stocking mask and hanging on the wall nearby is Peace's ingenious 'Ladder,' which he used to climb up to the bedroom windows he favoured. Thirteen pieces of 3in x 2in wood, each about 14in long and each hinged to the next by stout bolts. Peace was able to fold this equipment into a very small compass and carry it about in his violin case, taking it out and unfolding it when it was needed and is remembered as being one of the few murderers to write his own obituary:

'For that I don [*sic*], but never intended.'

4

THE ASHTON POISONING CASE

Ashton-under-Lyne, 1886

Mary Ann Hague was born in Bolton in 1847 but later moved to Park Bridge, on the boundary of Oldham and Ashton-under-Lyne, where she met the man who was to become her husband, Thomas Britland. They were married at St Michael's Church, Ashton, and by 1881 they had moved again and were living at 133 Turner Lane. By then, she and Thomas had two children, Elizabeth Hannah and Susannah, plus Thomas's daughter by an earlier marriage, also named Hannah, who later married and moved away.

Thomas changed his job several times during the years, eventually becoming a pub barman, a position that seemed to suit him, for he was a formidable drinker when he was in the mood for it, whilst his wife worked at Fisher's Mill, by the town centre. By 1886, they moved yet again to 92 Turner Lane and Mary Ann's nineteen-year-old daughter, Elizabeth Hannah, now worked at the mill with her. The younger girl, Susannah, aged eighteen, was in domestic service in Werneth, Oldham, at the home of a grocer, Mr Armitage, and lived in, although she did try whenever possible to come home to see her parents on her day off. To all intents and purposes, the Britlands seemed happy enough, although Mary Ann was prone to criticise her husband because of his drinking.

Since moving into Turner Lane, Mary Ann had made the acquaintance of the Dixon family, Thomas and Mary, who lived at No. 128. Thomas Dixon was born at Brighouses and married his wife in Halifax on the 11 April 1879, the couple coming to Ashton in July 1882, where Mr Dixon worked at Holmes's mill. Within a short time, Mary Ann and Mary Dixon were virtually inseparable, and in and out of each other's houses on a daily basis. Nobody saw anything wrong in this, it was a close community, times were hard and people got on a lot better if they stuck together. However, Thomas Britland did not seem so keen on the Dixons, especially the man of the house who, he said to his friends in the local drinking house, seemed always to be around whenever he returned from work. Mary Ann laughed this off and told her husband they were lucky to have such good friends in the neighbourhood.

The one blot on the landscape was mice – they overran 92 Turner Lane, a not unusual situation in the unsanitary terraced streets of any Lancashire mill town. She complained to her landlord, Mr Fielding-Oldfield, that the mice were eating her towels, her clothes and anything else they could get their teeth into and he suggested that the best thing to do would be to get a cat. Mary Ann did not think much of having an extra mouth in the house to feed and so she did what everybody else did in her situation, she went down to the local chemist's shop, Hirsts in Old Street, and bought packets of mouse powder, for which she had to sign the poisons book and provide evidence of identity. The mice seemed to like Harrison's Vermin Killer the best, a lethal concoction of strychnine and arsenic mixed with rice, which initially seemed to solve the problem. But the mice soon returned in ever-increasing numbers and Mary Ann was forced to return to Hirsts for another supply.

On Monday 8 March 1886, Elizabeth Hannah Britland came home in a good mood. She had taken a day off from work and had spent it with her boyfriend, William Davies. Her mind still full of thoughts of the enjoyable day she had spent with William, she did not have much appetite for her tea and only had a light supper, before going to bed at around 9.30 p.m., to be ready for work the following morning. Before long, she felt uncomfortable, a feeling which gradually grew into stomach pains, which got worse as the night wore on. Mary Ann boiled some water and filled a stone hot water bottle, which Elizabeth clutched to her painful stomach, but this did not seem to help much and she spent a wakeful night, occasionally screaming out as the pain racked her body. Mary Ann did what little she could to ease her daughter and next morning, early, she went round to a friend who lived nearby, Mrs Sophia Walker, to ask her if she would send one of her children for Dr Thompson. Mrs Walker then accompanied Mary Ann back to the house, where they found Elizabeth in great pain and crying out, 'Oh mother, hold my hands' and 'Oh Mrs Walker, do hold my legs.' Sophia stayed for about an hour, during which the unfortunate Elizabeth suffered a number of painful spasms.

It was not unusual to have stomach problems in those days: food preparation was unhygienic, there was no means of keeping food cold, other than by leaving it on the stone slab that was kept in the larder and the number of mice running around the house did not serve to improve matters. Moreover, the state of the medical art in 1886 meant that treatment was little more than basic remedies and mumbo jumbo and when Dr Thomson arrived, he was not surprised to find his patient in bed clutching her stomach and complaining of diarrhoea. He examined Elizabeth, knowing full well that there was very little he could give her that would be of any use and told Mary Ann that there was nothing to worry about and to keep her daughter in bed and continue to administer the hot water bottle.

He called again in the afternoon and found little improvement in his patient, who was now also complaining of a choking feeling in her throat. Dismissing this as hysteria, Thompson said that he would send a bottle of stomach medicine round and went on his way. Over the next hour, Elizabeth's condition grew worse and as convulsions once more racked her body, Mary Ann grasped her ailing daughter's hands and whispered soothing words to her.

Suddenly, there was a knock at the front door and Mary Ann hurried to open it, thinking that it might perhaps be Dr Thompson making a further visit, but found to her surprise and delight that it was her friend Mary Dixon standing there. Mary had heard about Elizabeth's illness and she had come to offer whatever help she could. Mary Ann welcomed her in and the two women rubbed the invalid's hands and feet and tried to get her to drink a mouthful of tea, but this only served to make the young girl worse and the convulsions returned.

At about three o'clock, the Britland's landlord, Mr Fielding Oldfield, who was a grocer with a shop in Turner Lane, called and helped them to administer a linseed poultice and towards evening, Elizabeth's symptoms seemed to subside a little. Mary Ann and her friend, by now exhausted with their efforts, hoped that the crisis was over but suddenly, at about nine o'clock in the evening, Elizabeth Hannah Britland died. A sobbing Mary Ann covered her dead daughter's face with a towel and waited, whilst Mrs Dixon went for the doctor. He came eventually and examined the corpse as it lay on the bed, all the while thinking about his diagnosis, which he eventually wrote on the death certificate as 'Bilious vomiting, convulsions and spasms of the heart.' Whether this diagnosis would meet with the approval of today's medical men is doubtful.

In the Lancashire mill towns of those days, the local community knew what to do when one of their number passed away. Two neighbours would process up the street, knocking on each door and asking for a contribution towards a communal wreath whilst word would be sent to the 'layer-out,' a local woman who for a few coppers would come to wash the dead body and prepare it for burial. In this case, it was Mrs Sarah Lord who knocked at the door early on the morning of 10 March and was shown into the dead girl's bedroom by a weeping Mary Ann Britland.

Mrs Lord, a widow, had been surprised to hear of Elizabeth Britland's death, as she had seen her in good spirits only two days before, but such occasions were not unusual and she set about her task of preparing the body. Mary Ann told her, rather brusquely Sarah thought, to prepare the body quickly before rigor mortis set in, and as she went about her task, Sarah was struck by the stiffness in the dead girl's fingers, something she put down to the agonies she had suffered in her last convulsions.

On Thursday 11 March, Mary Ann visited the office of Richard Mortimer, the agent for the Prudential Assurance Co., who had customers in virtually every house in Turner Lane. With little formality, Mortimer paid out £10, proceeds of Elizabeth's life policy, possibly the largest sum of money that Mary Ann Britland had ever had in her possession at one time. From there, she visited the undertakers to make arrangements for her daughter's funeral.

Despite the tragedy that had overtaken her family, Mary Ann was still concerned about the mouse problem and on 30 April, she asked a friend of hers, Mary Hadfield, if she would come with her to the chemists in order to buy more powders. This time, instead of going to Hirsts, she went to the shop of a Mr Kilvington, in Wellington Road, where she bought three 3*d* packets of 'Hunters Infallible Vermin and Insect Destroyer.' There might, perhaps, have been a warning on the packets pointing out that the contents would not only do away with vermin and insects, but a human being as well, containing as they did nearly two grains of strychnine. On the same day, Mary Ann called at the Mortimer's house and handed to Mrs Mortimer the sum of 1*s* 8*d* to cover her husband's 'Club money.' Mrs Mortimer was a little surprised as this was not the usual day for the insurance premium to be paid, but she realised that Mrs Britland had much on her mind and saw no reason to refuse the money, even though it was a few days early.

That evening, Thomas Britland came home late and exhausted, for after finishing his work, he had occupied himself in preparing his horse for the May Day parade, which was a local feature. He was tired and Mary Ann suspected that he had been drinking, but Thomas ate his supper and went straight off to bed. Next morning, seeing that a night's sleep had done little to revive her husband, Mary Ann sent for a doctor, this time Dr Charles Tucker, whom she told that her husband had not been sleeping well for weeks. She also confided that she suspected that he was drinking too much. When Tucker heard what Thomas Britland's daily consumption of beer was, he blanched, thinking to himself that Britland drunk more in a night than he did in a month!

Examining Thomas, Dr Tucker noticed that he was trembling and in a high state of nerves, but he put this down to delirium tremens, a not unlikely diagnosis considering the amount of drink that Britland tucked away on a regular basis. Doing what he could, the doctor left Thomas in the care of Mary Ann, who seemed to him to be very concerned about her husband's health.

However, apart from her husband, Mary Ann was still occupied with the mouse problem and went out to make a further purchase of Harrison's Vermin Killer, from Hirsts. This had the same two grains of strychnine in it as had the Infallible Vermin and Insect Destroyer, with the addition of 3.72 grains of arsenic, each a fatal dose for a human. A man named Waterhouse, who was in the shop at the time, saw what she was buying and commented that she should be sure to administer them scientifically and not in too large doses. Winking his eye, he commented, 'You will soon be in possession of the Club money.' Mary Ann turned on him, horrified, 'You don't suppose, for God's sake, that I would do that!' she screamed and Waterhouse beat a hasty retreat.

Back home, Mary Ann brought the hot water bottle into use again, but it seemed to be having little effect and Thomas lay in bed groaning, his feet twitching and his throat choking, occasionally vomiting into a bowl. Round about noon on 3 May, after seemingly starting to recover, Thomas took a turn for the worse and this time, Mary Ann sent for her faithful friends, the Dixons, who assisted her to rub Thomas's limbs, in which he had now lost most of the feeling. Mrs Dixon suggested that they should try a mustard bath, but Thomas had hardly got his feet into the mixture of mustard and hot water when he collapsed and, muttering a few indistinguishable words, expired in the arms of his weeping spouse.

Dr Tucker arrived and made the unlikely diagnosis of death by epilepsy, although so far as anyone knew, Britland had never suffered from the condition before. Thomas Dixon, having taken the news of Britland's demise to his former workplace, now offered to accompany the widow to collect the 'Club money,' an offer that she eagerly accepted. The couple promptly went to the offices of the Independent Order of Oddfellows to collect the cash. This was not the first time that Mrs Britland had been out on some errand with Thomas Dixon and one or two of the neighbours shook their heads silently and tutted, as they peered from behind the curtains drawn in sympathy for their deceased neighbour. Unfortunately, Mrs Britland had brought the wrong documents with her and there was nothing for it but for the couple to return home, thoughtfully splitting up as they approached Turner Lane, because as Dixon remarked to the cabman as he paid him off, 'People do talk so.'

At the second visit, everything was in order and after a visit to the offices of the Prudential as well, Mary Ann had in her handbag the total sum of £19 7s, more than enough to cover the funeral expenses and see her in funds for several months. For the next few days, she was fully occupied with preparations for the funeral and arranged with a Mrs Talent to clean the carpets and generally prepare the house. According to Mrs Talent's evidence at the subsequent trial, she had found no traces of mice activity whatsoever.

It was only after Thomas had been laid to rest that the reality of the situation began to sink in for Mary Ann. She was now on her own and the sole earner, apart from young Susannah who contributed what little she could afford, and she confided her worries about the future to her bosom friend Mary Dixon, who was now dearer to her than ever and who made every effort to comfort her friend and neighbour. Mary Dixon was indeed a true friend, for soon she made it clear to Mary Ann that she was welcome to come to stay at her home for as long as it took her to come to terms with the loss of two members of her family in such a short time.

On the 9 May, Mary Ann accompanied Thomas Dixon to a hat shop in Ashton, where a few months before, her late husband had bought a hat. The shop owner agreed to exchange it for one that would fit Dixon, charging them 5s and they left the shop with Thomas Dixon sporting his new headgear. On Thursday 10 May, Mary Dixon and her husband did some shopping and at 10 p.m., she arrived home on her own, leaving her husband to finish some business in the town. Somewhat to her surprise, she found the supper prepared and laid out waiting for their return and promptly slipped down to Mary Ann's house to invite her to share the repast that she had so kindly prepared for them. Once Thomas returned, about 10.30 p.m., they all sat down to eat, including Mrs Dixon's father, who had a room in the attic, and her unmarried daughter Selina Wolfenden, who also lived with them. The meal consisted of tea, bread and butter and a peculiar salad mix of cauliflower, cucumber, pickles and onions, almost certainly calculated to give them all indigestion before they went to their beds at nearly midnight. Mary Ann accepting an invitation to share Selina's room for the night.

After quarter of an hour, Mary Dixon began to suffer stomach pains and her husband got up to make her a hot drink, telling Mary Ann, who had appeared at their bedroom door, that his wife was ill. Judging from the sounds coming from the Dixons' bedroom, that was certainly the case and Mary thrashed about in considerable pain, clutching her abdomen. Whilst Mary Ann warmed some flannels to place on Mrs Dixon's stomach, Thomas Dixon went for Dr Thompson who arrived and administered a dose of opium to deal with the severe pain that Mary Dixon was now suffering. This seemed to do the trick and Mary's pain subsided, although she was still in considerable discomfort, her face a grotesque mask of contortions and her eyes showing a fixed stare. Thomas Dixon seems not to have paused to think that his wife was now exhibiting all the symptoms that had been shown by Elizabeth and Thomas Britland.

As the night went on, Mary Dixon's condition seemed to improve, but to the great consternation of the family and Mary Ann, she slid into unconsciousness and died at 5.50 a.m. on 14 May. Dr Thompson reappeared and made out the death certificate, again relying on Mary Ann's description of her friend's sufferings to certify that death was due to abdominal spasms. It must be remembered that the state of the medical art in late Victorian times was limited and such vague reasons for death as 'abdominal spasms' which could have meant anything and would be completely unacceptable on a death certificate today, were then perfectly in order. Barely thirty years before no fewer than four of Dr William Palmer's children had died in Rugeley, the cause of death being certified as 'convulsions.'

The 'layer-out' Mrs Lord arrived mid-afternoon to carry out her duties and Mary Ann again urged her to complete her duties before the corpse went stiff. Later, Mrs Lord was to mention to neighbours that she had found the dead woman's hands tightly clenched, as though in some terrible pain. In her long association with the care of dead bodies, she had rarely seen such a thing before, with the exception of the bodies of Elizabeth and Thomas Britland, which were still fresh in her memory.

Despite the death of his wife, Thomas Dixon felt able to visit his Club man Amos Perry straight away, to claim the sum of £19 17s 6d. Perry came back with him to the house, where Mary Ann Britland appeared to be in a frantic mood, crying out that the police had been there enquiring about Mary Dixon and wanting to know what Mary had eaten for her supper and how long she had been ill. They had demanded to see Mary's medicine and had examined the house and the back yard, before leaving. 'I don't care if a hundred coppers have been here,' snorted Thomas Dixon, 'I would rather have my Mary than the club money, any time.' Perry, who had been a silent witness to all this, pointed out quietly that there had now been three similar deaths in a short time in Turner Lane and so it was hardly surprising that the police were taking an interest. Mary Ann, in tears, sobbed, 'What's it got to do with them? Do they think we poisoned her?' It was some minutes before Mary Ann was calm enough to act as a witness to the forms Perry needed signing, certifying that the corpse upstairs was indeed that of Mary Dixon, but at length the business was completed and Amos Perry duly paid out the Club money on the following day.

It was later discovered that the reason why the Chief Constable, George Dalgliesh, had sent men round to the Dixon's house was an anonymous letter the police had received (which was never shown in evidence) pointing out the suspicious circumstances attached to the three recent deaths in Turner Lane. Dalgliesh also ordered a post-mortem on the deceased woman and an inquest.

In the meantime, Mary Ann was busying herself with the funeral arrangements, something with which she was now becoming familiar, and had asked a local coffee house owner, John Henry Law, to visit her at the Dixon's house, to arrange the supply of food for the funeral. Whilst this was being discussed, in the room where Mary Dixon's body lay, word reached them about the post-mortem, which was to be performed that very afternoon. Suddenly, Mary Ann turned to Mr Law and blurted out, 'Can they tell if a person has been poisoned?' Law, somewhat surprised at this outburst replied that he thought that they could. Mary Ann went on, 'Can they tell if they have had mouse powder?' and the even more surprised and now not a little worried Law stuttered that he thought that was indeed possible. Mary Ann, who was now obviously in need of a good lawyer by her side, went on, 'Can they tell if she had had it in tea?' which brought the same answer from her bewildered companion.

Mary Ann then admitted that she had bought a mouse powder at Kilvington's about a week ago, news which caused Law nearly to collapse. Now in a panic, he called Thomas Dixon, who was in an adjoining room, and in his presence exhorted her to repeat what she had just told him. By now, Mary Ann was beginning to realise that she had said far too much and refused to speak, so Law explained to Dixon what had transpired, including the purchase of the mouse powder. On hearing this news, Thomas Dixon went over to his wife's corpse and threw his arms round it, moaning, 'Oh Mary, if any person has given you poison, please tell me.' The corpse remained silent.

Law suggested that they should keep quiet about the mouse powder and Mary Ann told Thomas Dixon that it was within his power to have the post-mortem cancelled. 'You can prevent them opening her,' she told him and he replied, 'I cannot. I do not care if they cut her into little pieces.' Later that afternoon, the post-mortem was carried out in the same room and glass jars stood on the mantelshelf containing portions of the unfortunate Mary Dixon's organs. Other members of the Dixon family were now in the house and Mary Ann said to one of them, 'Oh, Mrs Dixon, Can they tell if she has had mouse powder and if she has had it in tea?' to which the startled Mrs Dixon, the stepmother of the dead woman, replied, 'Oh Mrs Britland, don't talk like that because it makes one suspicious.'

The result of the post-mortem, held on 17 May, was that there was nothing to show that Mary Dixon had died from natural causes. The glass jars and their grim contents were handed to analyst Mr Estcourt, who later found one thirtieth of a grain of arsenic and one tenth of a grain of strychnine in the contents. The police now issued orders for the exhumation and examination of the bodies of Elizabeth and Thomas Britland.

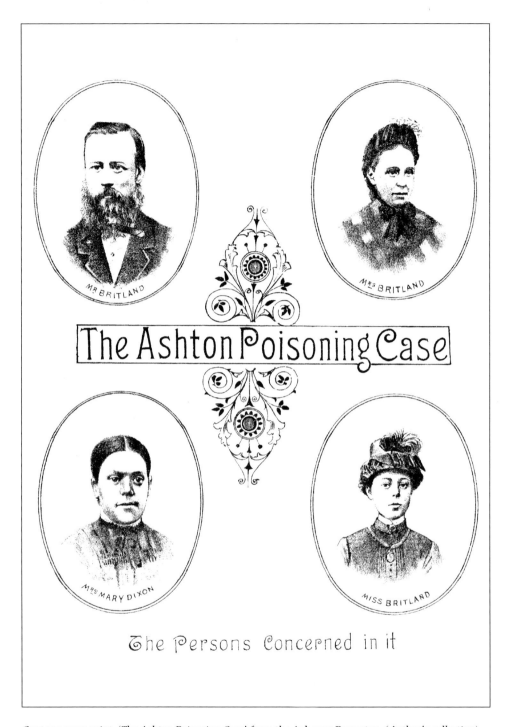

Contemporary print, 'The Ashton Poisoning Case' from the Ashover Reporter. *(Author's collection)*

On Tuesday 22 May Inspector Snell visited 92 Turner Lane and arrested Mary Ann Britland on a charge of murdering Mary Dixon and on suspicion of the murders of Elizabeth Hannah Britland and Thomas Britland, all by poison. 'Are they bringing that against me and all?' Mary Ann asked. 'I am innocent of that.' She was taken to the Town Hall in floods of tears and continued to weep bitterly when she was locked up in the cells. The *Ashton Reporter* commented that the only motive ascribed for the alleged crimes was that Mrs Britland sought to bring about a marriage between herself and Thomas Dixon, the husband of the deceased, and continued primly that this was, of course, purely a matter of surmise!

The next day, Mary Ann was taken before the magistrates on a charge of the wilful murder of Mary Dixon by administering poison. The Chief Constable, George Dalgliesh, prosecuted and Mr F.W. Bromley, a local solicitor, appeared for the defendant. Mr Dalgliesh told the court that Mary Ann Britland appeared on a very serious charge of wilful murder and of causing the death of Mrs Dixon by the administration of strychnine contained in vermin killer. Lewis Wolfenden, Mrs Dixon's father, gave evidence of his daughter falling ill and said that the accused was staying in the house at the time. He was followed by the pharmacist, Mr Kilvington who attested that he had supplied a packet of Hunters Vermin Killer to Mrs Britland and afterwards, William Henry Greenhalgh, assistant to Joseph Hirst, said that he had also supplied vermin killer to the accused. Mary Ann's solicitor then applied for bail, but this was strongly opposed by the prosecution and she was remanded in custody. On hearing this, Mary Ann appeared to fall into a half-faint, but she soon recovered herself and disappeared into the cells.

Several prominent members of local society wrote letters to the *Reporter* offering Thomas Dixon their condolences on the loss of his wife and he and what was left of his family had an escort of around eighty members of the Temperance movement when they next attended church. At midnight on 6 June the exhumation of the bodies of Thomas and Elizabeth Britland began and by quarter to four, well before the sun rose, two coffins lay unearthed side by side. These were then taken to the mortuary at Ashton Town Hall and at 10.15 a.m., an inquest was held in the Borough courtroom before Mr F. Price. After evidence of identification and brief details of the three deaths, the inquest was adjourned and at the subsequent Magistrate's hearing, Mary Ann was remanded to the Manchester Assizes on a charge of murder.

The indictment of Thomas Dixon as an accessory to murder having been quashed, her trial opened on Thursday 19 July before Mr Justice Cave. The story of Mrs Britland's familiarity with the Dixon family was recounted and the court buzzed with excitement when they heard about the hat that she had bought for the dead woman's husband.

The medical evidence was that Thomas Britland's body had been found to be in good order, including the liver (surprising, in view of his heavy drinking) and no trace of strychnine had been found, although there was about one tenth of a grain of arsenic present. This was not enough to constitute a fatal dose and it was

Thomas Britland's death certificate showing the true cause of death, which was initially shown as epilepsy. (Crown copyright)

an amount that could have come from contamination of the soil at the burial site, although no mention was made of this possibility.

Mr Law's evidence about his conversation with Mary Ann was particularly damning and he went on to say that Mary Ann had asked him if he thought that Mary Dixon had been poisoned. He had told her that he could not tell and Mrs Britland then asked if he had ever seen anyone who had been poisoned. 'Only one,' he said, 'and he swelled up and went black.' He told Mary Ann that the man had had a mouse powder, to which she replied, 'But Mary did not swell up!' 'Perhaps she did not have a full dose!' was Law's somewhat sinister reply.

This was followed by evidence that the analyst had found one thirtieth of a grain of arsenic in Mary Dixon's body, (again, nowhere near a fatal dose) and one tenth of a grain of strychnine. Prosecuting counsel, Mr Addison QC, made it clear to the jury that Mary Dixon had died of strychnine poisoning and said that the question was, if she died of poison, was she murdered? He then referred to the question of motive and pointed to the close and possibly intimate relationship the accused had had with the dead woman's husband. 'Firstly,' he said to the jury, 'she had to get rid of a daughter, then a husband, leaving her own house empty bar herself, and then she turned her attentions to Dixon's wife, thus leaving her free to carry on an even closer relationship with Thomas Dixon.' All this was, of course, pure supposition as even the QC had to admit that he had 'no means of entering the human heart and finding out what passions might be laying there.' The judge, however, made no attempt to reign in Adderley's suppositions, nor for that matter, did Mary Ann's defender, Mr Blair.

A prosecution witness, Mr Fielding Oldfield, told the court that he had known the Britland family for eight or nine years and had found them to be of good character all that time. He agreed that husband and wife had seemed on good terms with each other and that the children had been brought up properly. He said that the Britlands had rented the house in Turner Lane from him around the previous Christmas and that both the Britlands and the previous tenants had complained about the mice. Oldfield told the court that he had advised Mary Ann to get a cat, but she said that this would not be possible, as her husband kept a cage-bird. Oldfield's alternative suggestion was to use mouse powder.

The layer-out, Sarah Lord, said that she had found all three of the deceased unusually stiff when she attended to them, more so than any of the other corpses she had prepared. She told the court that when she began to wash Mrs Dixon, the deceased was warm underneath but began to discolour and she had great difficulty in taking off the dead woman's shift, as she went so stiff.

The court rose at five o'clock in the afternoon and resumed the following morning. There was a much greater demand for seats in the public gallery than there had been the previous day and by ten o'clock, the court was full and there were long queues outside. As on the previous day, Mary Ann Britland was allowed to sit in the dock and to those in the courtroom, she looked very composed although occasionally her complexion flushed. Lewis Wolfenden was the first witness and confirmed that Mr and Mrs Dixon were on good terms. When questioned by Mr Addison as to whether there were any mice in the house, he said indignantly that he had never seen one in his life, nor had he heard of any being in the Britland's home.

Dr Charles Thompson described how he had been called out on the night of 13 May to go and see Mrs Dixon and he described her symptoms, for which he prescribed belladonna and colocynth. He had asked his patient if she had eaten anything that might disagree with her and was told 'No.' He thought that she had been suffering from an attack of colic.

Susannah Britland gave her evidence seated and was obviously struggling with her emotions. She had often heard Mr Dixon say that he wished he had a wife like Mary Ann and also she had heard him say many times that he wished he had never known his wife and family. She also confirmed that she had heard her father grumbling about the number of times Thomas Dixon came to the house. She knew that there were mice in the house, although she knew nothing about the purchase of any mouse powder. 'You found a dead mouse yourself once,' challenged Mr Blair.

'Yes sir, but it was many months ago.'

'And your mother was particularly clean and industrious around the house?' asked Blair.

'Yes.'

'Unhappy if anything was out of order or dirty?'

'Yes.'

'She was also a very sober woman, was she?'

'Yes.'

Susannah was questioned closely about Thomas Dixon's comings and goings and she admitted that anything that had been said about this had been said in the presence of her sister and her young man. Her father had said many times that he did not care for Dixon coming, although she did not think that he had said this to Dixon's face.

Thomas Harris, physician, said that he and Dr Hamilton had made a post-mortem examination of the exhumed bodies of Elizabeth Hannah Britland and her father on 10 June and he found nothing in either body to account for death. 'Traces of rigor were still present in both bodies,' he said, 'and rigor mortis often remained longer after death from strychnine poisoning.' Later, Charles Estcourt told the court that he had examined the samples sent to him by Inspector Snell and found them to contain one-twentieth of a grain of arsenic. Once again, this amount of arsenic was far from being a fatal dose, but no attempt to point this out was made by the defence. No trace of strychnine had been found in either body, but this did not surprise him, as by the time of exhumation, the strychnine would have been fully absorbed.

The next witness was Dr Julius Dreschfield, Professor of Pathology at Victoria University. Agreeing that he had heard all the evidence as to the symptoms shown by Thomas and Elizabeth Britland, he confirmed that it was his opinion that they had died from the effects of Strychnia. If arsenic was mixed with the poison, the poisonous effect would be strengthened. Both the Britlands had exhibited spasms of the extremities of the body, twitchings in the fingers and pain in the abdomen and diarrhoea. It was also his opinion that Thomas Britland had received at least two doses of poison and that it was quite likely that Elizabeth had suffered the same. Both had shown signs of recovery from the first dose and had then relapsed, indicating that more poison had reached their systems.

Then came a surprise witness in the shape of Sergeant Joseph Nightingale. It was he who had taken Mrs Britland from Strangeways Prison to the Ashton Magistrate's hearing and he told the court that during the journey, Mary Ann had said to him, 'Do you think they will let him off today?' referring to Thomas Dixon. Nightingale immediately counselled her not to say anything more, but she went on, 'I suppose you have got an idea.' The sergeant replied, 'Some people seem to think he will get off,' to which his prisoner said, 'He has no right to get off, nor he won't if I could tell my mind. He ought to have been locked up all the time, same as me. It were him that led me into it and he wanted me to go away before I was locked up and he would go with me when the bother was over,' and then she repeated, 'Dixon will not get off when I tell my mind' and continued, 'I have done nothing to go away for and if I go away, people will think I am guilty, whether I am or not.'

It was then time for Mr Blair to do what he could to save his client from the gallows. 'No motive,' he said, 'has been given in court for the alleged crimes and if it is suggested that the accused killed for monetary gain, the amounts she actually received, although a not inconsiderable sum for a woman in her position, were as nothing compared to the loss of wages of Elizabeth and husband Thomas, who were both fit and well and would have been capable of bringing income into the house for years to come.' No evidence had been given to prove that there was anything but normal friendship between Mary Ann and Thomas Dixon and on the other hand, there was plenty to show that there was a very real friendship between Mary Ann and Mary Dixon and he pointed out how eager Mrs Dixon had been to give what help she could to her widowed friend, something that she would surely not have done if she had had any suspicion at all of a liaison between Mary Anne and her own husband.

Mrs Britland, said Mr Blair, had also good reason for buying the mouse powder, as there had been ample evidence presented to the court that mice were indeed a problem at 92 Turner Lane. She had even taken a friend with her on one purchase in order to act as a witness: would she have done this if the mouse powder were not merely for dispatching the vermin? It would be their duty, he told the jury, after most careful consideration, to say that the case had not been proved, as a capital case ought to be proved on behalf of the Crown.

The summing up of Mr Justice Cave was a long one. He gave the jury two questions to answer. Firstly, did Mary Dixon die in consequence of mouse powder? Secondly, if she did, did the accused administer it? He then went through the medical and chemical evidence, which showed that Mary Dixon had definitely died of strychnine poisoning, as well as the other two people concerned in the case. It was for the jury to decide if she had been given mouse powder by the accused and if they were not satisfied that Mrs Britland had given Mary the poison, then they must acquit her at once. On the other hand, if the jury thought that the deceased had died of the mouse powder, then they would have to ask themselves if the accused had the material and the opportunity. Mrs Britland, in buying six packets of mouse powder, had been in possession of a considerable amount of poison, which would have been sufficient to kill several thousand mice and she had had unlimited opportunities to administer it. Then there was the matter of her conversations with Amos Perry and Mrs Dixon, the stepmother: they were certainly suspicious.

His Lordship then told the jury that there was just a possibility that the powders were administered accidentally, although it was difficult to understand how the accident could have happened three times in such a short period. Apart from Mrs Dixon, there were four people present at that supper, Mary Ann Britland, Mr Dixon and his father and Selina, but only Mary Ann was known to have bought mouse powder.

The jury retired, returning after two hours to tell the judge that despite the evidence, they were convinced that Thomas Dixon had somehow been involved in the murder of his wife, a theory which the judge dismissed peremptorily. A few minutes later, the jury were back again, this time with a verdict of 'Guilty,' at which Mary Ann Britland burst into tears. When asked by the Judge if she had

Mary Ann Britland on the scaffold, from a contemporary print. (Author's collection)

anything to say why sentence of death should not be passed on her, the distraught woman replied, 'No, my Lord, I have not. I have administered nothing at all to Mary Dixon, nothing whatever.'

The judge looked at her sternly. 'It was a murder committed under circumstances of great cruelty. There is no kind of murder that is worse than administering poison, especially when it is administered by one person of a household to another who sheltered her. He then pronounced sentence of death, which sent the woman in the dock into hysterics and her cries were heard throughout the courtroom as she was taken down to the cells.

A petition was raised but was unsuccessful and as the days went past, Mary Ann's condition became worse and she sat in the condemned cell weeping and wailing and asking for God's mercy. The hangman, James Berry, said that her cries on the way to the scaffold were heart rending and heard all over Strangeways Prison. As she approached the scaffold, supported by two wardresses, she was crying out, 'Oh! Oh! Dear me!' and as she stood on the trap, she screamed, 'God save me! Oh Lord have mercy on me!'

At the last moment, male warders replaced the two wardresses accompanying the by now almost unconscious woman and Berry pulled the lever, sending Mary Ann Britland 7ft down to her doom. She was the first woman to be hanged at Strangeways and her death was instantaneous.

5

THE STRANGEWAYS MURDER

Strangeways Gaol, Manchester, 1888

Twenty-eight-year-old John Jackson, alias Edward Graham, Charles Wood Firth and several other names, was already a hardened criminal when he appeared at Salford Quarter Sessions on 9 April 1888, charged with housebreaking at Eccles on 29 March. The break-in with which he was charged had availed him little, just a signature stamp, a money box and twopence, the property of a Salvation Army Captain named Alfred Poynter.

Jackson was of medium height, with fresh complexion, brown hair and brown eyes and he had a slight deformity on the forefinger of his left hand, apart from which he looked no different than hundreds of honest Manchester artisans following their trade. When Jackson followed an honest occupation, which was not often, it was that of plumber. It was, perhaps, his ordinary appearance that enabled him to wheedle his way into properties on one pretext or another and then rob them and for some reason never satisfactorily explained, he seems to have had a preference for property owned by members of the Salvation Army. It is said that his idol was Charlie Peace and like Peace, he was in and out of prison and had been last in Armley Gaol, serving six months, before being released in June 1885.

Just prior to his attempt to break into Captain Poynter's house, he had aroused the curiosity of a local constable, PC Crowther, who, by arrangement with Poynter, hid himself in the house that evening and awaited developments. Noises at the front door told him that someone was trying to force an entrance, but after trying unsuccessfully for a few minutes, the person moved round to the back of the house and shortly afterwards, came the crash of broken glass, as the kitchen window was smashed.

John Jackson, from a contemporary drawing.
(Author's collection)

Crowther kept still, whilst Jackson edged his way carefully through the broken pane and began to search for valuables. The constable waited a little longer, to give the intruder time to collect items that could be used in evidence against him and then pounced. After a brief struggle, he put the handcuffs on Jackson and took him off to the police station, where it was found that he was in possession of two jemmies, or crow bars. Whilst in custody, Jackson obviously worked out that he had been caught bang to rights and that there was no point in fighting the case, so he pleaded 'Guilty' to the charge and received six months with hard labour. Without further ado, he was transported to nearby Strangeways Gaol to do his stretch.

Strangeways, in Southall Street, Manchester, had been built to replace the New Bailey Prison in Salford, the scene of the dispatch of the Manchester Martyrs, which had closed in 1868, just a year after. Strangeways was designed by Alfred Waterhouse, using the radial system and was built to take approximately 1,000 prisoners. Being new, the prison was considered to be the epitome of what prisons should be, although whether this was a sentiment that occupied the minds of its inhabitants is doubtful. Behind the impressive outer walls, a 234ft tower, used for heating and ventilation, became a local landmark that still exists today.

Amongst the staff at the prison was the matron, Elizabeth Little, who occupied a house within the precincts, the entrance to which was from the prison yard. One Saturday morning, on the 19 May 1888, the matron reported an escape of gas in one of her bedrooms and the Governor arranged for Jackson, in view of his plumbing experience, to be detailed to fix it. Accompanied by Assistant Warder Sutherland, Jackson went to the matron's house as ordered and the Governor, Major John William Preston, was later to say that he had seen the two men engaged in the work. On 21 May, the Chief Warder, Silas Denbow, received orders to replace Warder Sutherland with Assistant Warder Ralph Dyer Webb, as he needed Sutherland for other duties. Webb, who was forty-five years old, had been in the prison service for nine years and was considered by his superior officers to be steady, quiet and a good officer.

Webb and his charge went to the matron's house and at 5 o'clock in the afternoon, the work not being finished, Warder Webb assured the Matron that the gas leak had been effectively stopped and that the two of them would return the following day to complete the job, which they duly did on the Tuesday afternoon. Matron Little said that she saw the two men in her kitchen and later in the bedroom at about twenty minutes to four, after which they came down to the scullery, where the gas meter was situated. Jackson did something to the meter and they then went upstairs for the final time.

Matron Little remained in the kitchen for six or seven minutes and then went into her sitting room, which was directly underneath the room where the gas leak had occurred. As she did so, she heard an unusual rumbling sound overhead, like the drawing of a heavy piece of furniture across the floor. Slightly alarmed, although all the windows of her house were heavily barred, she went up to the bedroom but found the door fastened against her. Taking hold of the handle, she shook the door twice, shouting, 'Open the door' and a voice from inside the room called out, 'All right.' The Matron was by now thoroughly alarmed. 'All is not right!' she shouted and rattled the door once more. 'This door should not be locked.'

Stumbling down the stairs, she rushed outside into the yard, meeting Assistant Warder William Young, who was actually on his way to her house to relieve Webb, to enable him to get his tea. Young followed her into the house and went upstairs to the bedroom. Calling for assistance from two other warders, they forced the door open and found the body of Warder Webb on the floor, lying on his left side, with his feet pointing towards the door. The furniture did not appear to have been moved, except for a chair, which had been placed underneath a gaping hole in the ceiling and of Jackson, there was no sign. When asked, the matron confirmed that the hole had not been there when she was last in the room and that Warder Webb and Jackson had appeared to be on friendly terms whilst the work was being done. Webb was thought to be a most kind-hearted man, popular with everyone and no-one had reckoned on this sort of incident happening.

Aid was brought for the injured Webb, who was now unconscious. The prison doctor, Charles Braddon, examined him and saw that he was suffering from a contused and lacerated scalp wound on the left side of the head, at the back. The wound was rather more than 2in in length and reached to the bone. Webb stirred and opened his eyes. 'Where are my boots?' he muttered and Braddon saw that the man's prison boots were scattered on the other side of the room. Webb spoke again. 'Where is the plumber?' and then lapsed back into unconsciousness. When the injured man came round, Braddon asked him where the man was who had been working with him. 'Here in the room,' Webb said, falteringly.

'And how did you come by your injury?'

'I fell,' said the injured warder and became unconscious again. He was taken to the prison hospital, where he died at about quarter past six in the evening.

Dr Braddon performed a post-mortem and his report, at the National Archives, states that beyond the head wound, there were no other external marks of violence. On opening the head, he found a fracture of the skull extending from the left side, corresponding to the external wound and extending downwards to the base of the skull. There was a large effusion of blood at the base of the brain, caused by the rupture of blood vessels consequent on the fracture of the skull. The body was otherwise that of a healthy man and cause of death was compression of the brain. In the doctor's opinion, the fracture would have required great violence and he did not think that a fall in the bedroom could have caused it. A heavy hammer, later found by Warder James Sammons on the lead guttering of the roof of the matron's house, was found to be the weapon. He also discovered a chisel near the chimney, alongside the hole in the roof.

It seemed obvious that Jackson had attacked the warder unawares, possibly seeking only to stun the man whilst he made his escape through the ceiling, an immediate search of the prison failed to disclose his whereabouts. Subsequently, it was discovered that Jackson, on getting into the roof space, had removed some of the slates from the roof of the matron's house, which abutted onto Southhall Street and had made a desperate and daring descent from the roof, via a downspout, seemingly unnoticed by anyone.

Warders who knew Jackson were despatched to search the surrounding streets and the Manchester City Police were informed, although oddly enough they were not warned about the seriousness of the matter until some hours later, after Webb had died. The famous Manchester policeman, Jerome Caminada, became involved and acting on information supplied by an informant, he went to Oldham with a posse of officers, but with no result. Caminada warned the Oldham police that Jackson would be likely to break into houses, looking for food and a change of his prison clothes and sure enough, within twenty four hours, reports were coming in of two successful burglaries in the district and two failed ones. A Mr Taylor of Park Road, Oldham, complained that his house had been entered and he was missing a black worsted Chesterfield overcoat, a white linen jacket and a brown tweed vest. A stone bottle containing half a gallon of porter and a quantity of cigars had also gone. The second successful burglary was at the house of Thomas Wood, another Salvation Army Captain, who lived at 8 Cromwell Street, Oldham. It is not known how Jackson

Strangeways Prison. The Matron's house, scene of the murder and Jackson's escape, was further along the curtain wall and has since been demolished. (© A. Hayhurst)

discovered the Salvation Army connection, but it seems likely that when he had been at large before, he had sought assistance from the religious organisation and taken careful note of any information he gained from the unsuspecting charity workers. In fact, Wood's house had been broken into once before and it is quite likely that Jackson was the culprit on each occasion. On leaving for the second time, Jackson cheekily left a note which said, 'Goodbye, Captain. Though lost to sight, to memory dear. Yours truly, Shakespeare!'

Captain Wood lost a tweed coat and £11 6s in money and to add insult to injury, he happened to have the keys to the Salvation Army Citadel in the house, which Jackson took and used to let himself in. He evidently stayed there for some time, as police later found the empty bottle of porter and some partly smoked cigars. The keys to the premises had been thrown into the fireplace and when Jackson eventually moved on, he left behind a heavy hammer and three different sized screw drivers, which had been the proceeds of another robbery.

The *Oldham Standard* carried a note of the burglary and described how Jackson had made a supper for himself, consisting of bread and butter, cheese and marmalade. A reporter asked the unhappy Salvation Army captain if Jackson had also obtained the bottle of porter from his premises. A scandalised Captain Wood replied, 'Oh no! We keep nothing of that sort here.'

Jackson's escape, from a contemporary illustration. (Author's collection)

The burglary had first been discovered by a neighbour, Mr Dunkerley, who was going out to work when he noticed the back gate to Captain Wood's house was open and that a window had been broken. He roused Captain Wood, who throughout the whole episode had been asleep upstairs in bed. The intruder had actually entered the bedroom next to the one in which Captain Wood was sleeping and opened a box, which contained the sum of money he had taken. Obviously, Captain Wood was a heavy sleeper!

The search continued and both the Salford and Liverpool docks were thoroughly examined. Notices were sent to police stations country-wide, although neither the Manchester police nor the prison authorities had a photograph of Jackson. He had reportedly been seen in several public houses in the Oldham district and the stolen overcoat was eventually recovered from the front of the Jolly Carter beerhouse in Lees Road. A pawnbroker at Lees informed the police that Jackson had come into his shop that morning and had pawned another overcoat.

A facsimile of a contemporary booklet. (Courtesy of Alan and Marie Elmer)

He was able to give the police a good description of the man and the clothes he was wearing, which included brown ribbed trousers, slack black jacket with a white linen jacket underneath, brown and red mixture tweed vest, cap with two peaks, white handkerchief round the neck and was wearing a pair of well polished boots. Several arrests of men fitting this description were made, but all proved to be false alarms.

On Saturday morning, the daily papers announced that the fugitive had been caught in Dewsbury, although Jerome Caminada had already seen the man in custody there and had ascertained that he was not Jackson. Other reports of Jackson's capture came in from Wakefield, Stockport and Wolverhampton, but none were correct. Jackson remained at large for several weeks, but was eventually spotted and arrested in Bradford, after a trail of burglaries. His trial took place at Manchester Assizes on Friday 13 July, an unlucky day for Jackson if ever there was one. It was a short hearing, during which Jackson pleaded 'Not Guilty' and told the court, 'I have no witnesses.'

Mr Justice Grantham.
(Author's collection)

Manchester Assize Courts.
(Author's collection)

Executioner James Berry.
(Author's collection)

Frederick Liggins, Artisan Warder at the prison confirmed that he had control of any instruments and tools needed at the gaol and that the heavy hammer found in the bedroom was normally kept in the Engineer's office when not otherwise needed. He also confirmed that it was the only one of its kind in the prison. Evidence from the Matron and several prison officers followed and after hearing what little could be said on Jackson's behalf, Mr Justice Grantham summed up and the jury left to consider their verdict. It took them just six minutes to bring in a finding of 'Guilty' after which the judge donned the black cap and pronounced the death sentence.

Despite the despicable nature of his crime, more than 20,000 people signed a petition for Jackson's reprieve but the Home Secretary, Henry Matthews, had little difficulty in refusing any commutation of sentence and on the morning of 7 August 1888, at 8 a.m., Executioner James Berry entered Jackson's cell. It may be that Berry took more satisfaction than normal in this execution, as he had actually known Warder Webb, who had been his aide on several occasions when he was called to the prison to follow his calling. He found Jackson deeply contrite, protesting to the last that he had only intended to stun the unfortunate man and the condemned man died with a prayer on his lips. Webb's widow was allowed a pension of £15 a year, plus £5 for her child, which was augmented by a further £145 from public subscription.

6

A NASTY SHOCK!

Oldham, 1891

Alfred William Turner, twenty years old and 5ft 3in tall, had a reputation for being a wastrel. Hardly ever in work, when he found employment, he was never long in it, although currently, he was working as a labourer at Messrs Platt's mill, a prosperous local factory, known for paying good wages. He had also had a run-in with the Oldham police which did nothing for his reputation, so it was hardly surprising that young Mary Ellen Moran, only just turned eighteen, found his advances unwelcome. Her friends warned her that he would never make a good husband and told her that she should have nothing to do with him.

Mary, a mill hand, was an orphan and had been lodging, for about a fortnight, with a friend in Back Hope Street, Oldham. Despite her protestations to Turner that she wanted nothing to do with him, he persisted and on occasion, even said that he wanted to marry her. Her reply was always that he should not come near her again. However, despite her constant rejection of him, Turner suspected that Mary Ann was not entirely averse to his approaches and on 29 March 1891, he turned up at her lodgings and managed to persuade the girl to go for a walk with him to the neighbouring woods, near Woodstock Mill.

The next anyone knew of the couple was when Alfred Turner burst into the police station, shouting that they had been attacked. That was self-evident, because Turner's hands and clothes were covered in blood and he was in such an agitated state that PC Michael Conway at first thought that he had been drinking. Trying his best to calm the distraught Turner down, he managed to extract from him the fact that the young couple had been walking in the woods, when they were set upon by two men and savagely attacked. Turner had no explanation for this, but showed Conway his own injuries and said that he thought that Mary Ellen had suffered as much, if not more. In fact, he said repeatedly that he thought Mary was dead.

Turner's injuries did not seem to the constable all that serious, especially considering the amount of blood on him, but Turner explained that he had tried to take the injured Mary Ellen up in his arms and that a large amount of the blood on his clothes was probably hers. He was certain that when they went to the woods where Mary Ellen lay, they would find her dead and he believed that the attackers had cut the girl's throat.

Together, Turner and Conway set off back to the scene of the attack and as they approached, they found a shawl on the ground. 'That's her shawl,' said Turner, 'She can't be far away.' Hurrying on, they came across Mary Ellen, who to Turner's great surprise and no doubt shock, was far from dead, leaning against the mill wall, with blood pouring from her throat. 'She's not dead after all, Thank God,' said Turner as they raced towards her. Hearing them approaching, the injured girl turned and tried to grab hold of the constable's sleeve, at the same time struggling to say something, which the constable was unable to hear clearly. Turner turned back, saying that he would go for assistance, but was prevented from doing so by PC Conway, who insisted that he should help him to get the girl to a place of shelter as quickly as possible.

Together, the two men lifted the injured girl gently and carried her to a nearby cottage, where they sat her in a chair and attempted to staunch the flow of blood. Conway bent down low over the recumbent girl and asked in a hoarse voice if she knew who had attacked her. Unable to speak, Mary Ellen lifted her hand and pointed at Turner. 'I understood that two men attacked you,' said Conway. The girl tried to shake her head and again pointed at Turner, who protested long and loud that he had not done anything. 'It was two men that attacked us,' he shouted and Conway held up his hand to silence him. 'I'll take a statement from you in due course,' said the policeman and then duly cautioned him, whilst all the while, Turner repeated that his story was true. 'The girl is still indicating that you attacked her,' said Conway.

'No I didn't,' repeated Turner. 'It was two men, I tell you.'

'Well, I'm arresting you for the assault and you'll get a chance to tell your part of the story in due course,' said Conway, producing his handcuffs. Leaving the injured Mary Ellen in the care of the owner of the cottage, and promising him that he would get further help as quickly as possible, Conway took the still protesting Alfred Turner back to the police station and locked him up.

At five o'clock the following morning, PC Conway retraced his steps to the cottage and found signs of a struggle, including a pool of blood, near the mill. Arriving at the nearby railway line, he found more blood on the crossing gates and surrounding gravel. Meanwhile, Mary Ellen Moran had been taken to Oldham Hospital, where she lay in a grave condition. There, she was visited by Mr John Hargraves Knott, Clerk to the Oldham magistrates, who formed the opinion that the girl had not long to live, even though she was still conscious. Explaining to the girl that she was badly wounded and probably dying, he took from her a Dying Disposition, during which she slowly raised her hand, as if to grasp Knott's throat and whispered, 'He cut my throat.' The effort of making the statement exhausted the poor girl and she died shortly afterwards. The charge against Turner was now murder.

At the Coroner's inquest, the jury returned a verdict of wilful murder against him and he was taken before the Oldham magistrates for the committal hearing. For the first time since he had been detained, Turner now had the benefit of legal representation, who took up the only line of defence available to him and announced that Turner had been insane at the time of the incident. Throughout the hearing, Turner sat quietly and listened attentively to the evidence and then it was his turn to go into the witness box. To everyone's surprise, and despite efforts from his counsel to persuade him otherwise, Turner insisted on making a complete confession to the crime. His only excuse, he told the court, was that the girl he had hoped to marry told him that she wanted nothing more to do with him, after he had accused her of going out with another man. She had vehemently denied this and in a fit of rage, he had attacked and mortally wounded her. He made no explanation as to how or why he was carrying the murder weapon on what was supposed to be a romantic walk in the woods.

Turner was remanded for trial, which began at Manchester Assizes on Wednesday 29 April 1891 in front of Mr Justice Wright. Although it must have been a nasty shock for Turner when he and PC Conway came on Mary Ann Moran and found she was still alive, he kept his composure in the court as his counsel did everything he could to convince the jury that the accused man was not responsible for his actions due to hereditary insanity. The prosecution said that whilst Turner had been incarcerated at Strangeways Gaol, he had been under the scrutiny of the prison doctor, who testified that although Turner was undoubtedly of weak intellect, there was no evidence to show that he was anything but completely sane.

In his final speech, Mr Hamilton for the defence told the jury that it would be idle for him to protest that the accused had not done the deed for which he was now being tried. It was a most cruel act, he said, but there could be no doubt that Turner was deeply in love with the young woman and equally obvious that she did not fully reciprocate his affections. There was a history of insanity in the family and his mother had given evidence that his birth had been a very difficult one. She also said that the doctor who delivered him had told her that it would have been better if her son had died at birth and that he would probably cause her a load of trouble before he reached the age of twenty-one. Taking all this into consideration, he urged the jury to believe that the prisoner's heart, hand and mind had not acted in unison and that the act of murder had been involuntary and for which he was not responsible.

Summing up the case, the judge cautioned the jury that they must not consider acquitting the accused man merely because he was weak minded. If the prisoner did the act, knowing at the time what he did, their duty was clear. The jury took the judge's words to heart and they were away for only a few minutes before returning with a verdict of 'Guilty'. They did, however, add a rider, recommending mercy on account of Turner's family history of insanity, which before passing sentence of death, the judge said would be passed on to the appropriate authority.

Turner was taken back to Strangeways to await execution and passed his time writing to friends and relations, discussing the crime and acknowledging his guilt, which he put down to his bad temper. An appeal on the grounds of temporary insanity failed and the execution date was set for 19 May. During most of the time he had been confined, Turner had shown little emotion and had not expressed any regret for taking the life of an innocent young girl, he listened carefully to the ministrations of the Revd Draeper, but made no statement of any kind. During his last night on earth, Turner slept soundly, waking up twice for a few minutes before settling down again. He was wakened at 6 a.m. and again listened quietly to the Revd Draeper before taking a breakfast of bread and butter and tea. At 8 a.m., the prison bell commenced to toll and the executioner, James Berry, entered the condemned cell.

The condemned man submitted quietly to the pinioning and then followed a procession to the scaffold, led by Berry and including the prison surgeons, Drs Edwards and Paton and the acting Under-Sheriff, Mr Wilson. Six warders made up the rear. Waiting for them on the scaffold, some 20yds away from the condemned cell, were the Governor of the prison, Major Preston and Chief Warder Godfrey. Three pressmen had also been allowed to be present and they stood below the scaffold, with another group of warders.

Turner carried his head on his chest, understandably looking downcast and he appeared to be weeping. 'Forgive me, my God,' he said as he stepped under the beam. Cap and noose being fixed, he just had time to exclaim, 'Give my love to my mother,' before Berry pulled the lever and Turner dropped 6ft 9in to his death. This appeared to be instantaneous and painless. Outside the prison, the event appeared to have caused little concern and only a few people were waiting outside for the black flag to be hoisted. At the subsequent inquest, held later that morning, Mr John Edwards, prison surgeon, said that death had been caused by strangulation by hanging. This may have been merely a manner of speaking or he may have been indicating that Turner's neck had not been broken by the fall and that he took some minutes to die. The official report stated that the execution had gone off without incident.

7

MURDERED FOR
18 PENCE

Forty-one-year-old Frederick Ballington lived with his wife Ellen Ann at 143 Gladstone Street, Glossop, where together they ran a butcher's shop. Fred, as he was usually known, was the youngest of ten children and was born in Derby on 11 August 1867. Both Fred's parents died within weeks of one another when he was eleven and together with two of his brothers, he was sent to live with one of his married sisters. He had known Ellen Ann, who was a few months older than him, since he was a school boy and they married on Christmas Day 1885, already having one child, with another on the way. Fred, who was 5ft 1in tall and of stocky build, followed the occupation of 'brush maker.'

When the new baby arrived, he was named Samuel William, as it was a family tradition going back several generations that the first son was always called Samuel. Two more daughters followed and in 1898, the family moved to Glossop. Fred initially worked for Mr W. Shreeves, a butcher who had several shops in the area, but within a short time Fred had set himself up in a tiny house, 143 Gladstone Street, which had been converted to a shop in one of the two front rooms. There were two bedrooms, one occupied by Fred and Ellen and the other by the two daughters, and Samuel William camped out on the back landing.

Although the shop gave them a reasonable living, Fred Ballington was not good with money and on occasions he drank to excess, something that his wife objected to vociferously. Although he had been known to stay sober for as long as two years at a time, the local newspapers record him appearing at the Magistrate's Court on several occasions, for drunkenness and violent behaviour. It was hardly surprising therefore that the marriage was not a happy one and Ballington frequently left the family home, after quarrelling with his wife. People who knew her described her as

No. 143 Gladstone Street, Glossop, as it is today. The butcher's shop portion was to the right of the door. (© A. Hayhurst)

being a well-built woman, slightly taller than her husband and of quite handsome appearance, but also as being 'strapping and forceful.'

Sometime in April 1908, the quarrelling grew so bad that Fred was thrown out of the house, after his drinking grew more than his wife and their son, Samuel William, could stand. He found lodgings in White Street, Hulme, Manchester with Mrs Elizabeth Palin, who was later to say that although he occasionally came home slightly under the influence of drink, she had never known him drunk. He always seemed to her to be a nice sort of man, always quite rational, sensible and good tempered and so far as she was concerned, he had never shown any signs of mental instability.

Whilst lodging with Mrs Palin, he obtained casual labouring jobs at the Water Street abattoir, a place he knew well, as for years he had made regular trips there on a Monday to order meat for the shop. However, this casual work was ill paid and not regular and Ballington had great difficulty in making enough to keep body and soul together. On Monday 18 May 1908, he travelled to Glossop and appeared at the Gladstone Street shop, pleading that he had no money and asking to stay the night. Evidently, although Mrs Palin seemed to like him, she drew the line at putting him up free of charge and made it clear that if there was no rent, there was no room.

Instead of asking him to come in, Ellen gave him a small sum of money, which was just enough to get him a roof over his head for the night and the next day, he was back again, asking for money. This time, Ellen refused point blank and perhaps knowing from previous experience that his wife meant what she said, Ballington went away without arguing. Somehow, he found his way back to central Manchester, where he spent an uncomfortable night without a roof over his head.

Ellen had taken over the Monday morning visits to the abattoir, and knowing this, when he was not living at home, Fred would put in an appearance and exchange a few words with her. He would also usually walk her back to catch the Glossop train from London Road station (Now Piccadilly), a practice to which his wife did not seem to object. On 21 May, young Samuel Ballington visited the abattoir on business, and Fred took the opportunity to draw him to one side and plead with him to ask Ellen if she would give him some more money, as he wanted to go to Blackpool to find work. Whether Samuel passed on this message or not is not clear, but the likelihood is that his mother was by now completely disenchanted with her dissolute husband and was in no mood to give him anything.

PRISONER AT THE POLICE COURT.

"The Sooner they Hang me the Better"

Fred Ballington, from a contemporary newspaper. (Author's collection)

On the following Monday 25 May, Ellen Ballington took the train from Glossop to Manchester as usual, and made her way to the Abattoir. After transacting her business there, Fred Ballington appeared and the two talked together, to all appearances amicably enough. They walked to the shops in Oldham Street, where Ellen made one or two purchases and then Ellen went into Lord's Restaurant on her own to have lunch, leaving her husband outside. It seems clear that Fred's wife had no intention of wasting any more money on her husband, but when she had finished her lunch, she found Fred Ballington outside, still waiting for her. The couple walked to the fish market on Deansgate and Ballington again broached the subject of money to enable him to go to Blackpool. Ellen refused point blank, although the two kept together and caught a tram from Deansgate back to Water Street, where they went into the Ellesmere Hotel for a drink. Each had a glass of bitter, Ellen stubbornly insisting that her husband should pay for his own. Again, Ballington pestered his wife for money, this time asking for 3s and again she refused, but possibly to stop Fred's persistent approaches, she told him that when they got to London Road station, she would 'see what she could do.'

Ballington accepted this and went his own way, reappearing at London Road station at around 5 p.m. Despite her earlier statement, Ellen had spent the time on her own mulling over the situation and by the time Fred appeared, she was no longer of a mind to hand over any money. Seeing him coming, she went into the refreshment room, leaving her husband outside. When she came out, he was still there and the couple walked along the platform to where the Glossop train was standing, passing PC32 George Hebden, of the Railway Police, who knew them both quite well and was used to seeing them together. Fred had yet again asked for 3s and the two of them were arguing, and according to the constable, Ballington appeared to be using abusive language to his wife, although the policeman could not hear what was being said. However, he was certain that Mrs Ballington was holding her own in the argument and that she did not look flustered, whereas her husband was white with passion. The couple went on along the platform and PC Hebden continued on his patrol.

They were also seen by Alfred Milnes, a railway guard, who knew the Ballingtons and according to Milnes, Fred Ballington looked very upset, but he saw the couple walk to the end of the train and then sit down on a seat on the platform for a few minutes, before Ellen Ballington rose to board the train. Milnes then went to the front of the train and started to close the carriage doors.

At this time, the final compartment was empty, apart from Walter Clitherow Smith, a managing engineer from Urmston, who was reading a newspaper. He heard a man say, 'Don't go in there. There's a gentleman in.' and a woman replying, 'I shall,' and she proceeded to get into the carriage and sat down in a corner seat, next to the platform, facing the engine. Her male companion stood with one foot on the platform and the other on the step.

Smith, not wishing to appear nosy, buried his head in his newspaper and heard the man say, 'Lend me a few shillings,' or 'Come, lend me a shilling or two,' to which the woman replied, 'No, I won't.' The man asked again, raising his voice a little and the woman at last took out her purse and handed something to the man, who looked at it and said, 'Eighteen pence is no good to me. I must have something to get there. I need to look for a job. Just give me a few more shillings.'

'No, I won't. I gave you the other,' the woman retorted, 'Your trouble is that you're lazy. I have to work hard for the money I get. I keep the children. You go and work, you are idle.'

By this time, other people were getting into the carriage, despite which the man persisted with his request. He could now be heard by everyone in the carriage and suddenly got in and sat down by the woman, grabbing her in a rough embrace. The woman tore herself away from his grasp. 'How dare you,' she almost spat at him. The man stood up and looked down at her. 'It's now goodbye,' he said, 'and goodbye for ever' and turned to go back on to the platform. 'You're nought but a scamp,' the woman shouted after him. The man halted and came back into the carriage. 'No I'm not,' he said and caught hold of her again. By this time, Walter Smith was so alarmed that he opened the nearest carriage door, which was on the opposite side of the train to the platform and jumped out onto the line, intending to climb into the next carriage. Looking up, he saw the man with what appeared to be a knife at his own throat and heard a woman scream.

Frank Margrave, a partner in a hay and straw business, was also sitting in the carriage and had been watching the events without interfering. When the man tried to kiss his woman companion, Margrave hid behind his newspaper in embarrassment, but on hearing the woman scream, he looked up and saw that she was bleeding from a wound on her cheek. He at once got out of the compartment and informed a railway porter, who was on the platform.

A clerk, Reginald Shaw, was also in the compartment and like the other two men, gradually became aware of the seriousness of the argument between the couple. After watching the struggle, he heard a scream and was alarmed to see his fellow passenger, Smith, jump out of the carriage onto the line. Suddenly, Shaw saw the man standing in the carriage doorway with what he later claimed appeared to him to be a pistol, which the man was trying to push down his shirt. Not sure whether the pistol was intended to be pointing at the man or at him, Shaw followed the example of Walter Smith and jumped out of the compartment on to the platform and went to a carriage further along for assistance, but found it was full of ladies. Thinking that discretion was perhaps the better part of valour, Shaw sat down on a vacant seat, much to the chagrin of the passengers in the 'Ladies Only' compartment.

Meanwhile, the scream and the subsequent movements had attracted the attention of several passengers, amongst them a commercial traveller named George Ogden. He had heard a scream coming from the next compartment and looking out of the window, could see Walter Smith in the four-foot way, waving his arms about in distress. Ogden and several others went into the compartment, where they saw

Ellen Ballington in a seated position, her clothing covered in blood, which seemed to be coming from a wound in her neck. Fred Ballington pushed past him through the door and on to the platform and Ogden saw that his hands were also covered in blood and there was blood on his collar and tie. A knife with a blood stained blade lay on the floor.

Attracted by the commotion, Guard Milnes came up and, seeing the condition of Ellen Ballington, immediately went off to summon an ambulance. He also alerted PC Hebden, who was further down the platform. Fred Ballington was now beginning to walk away, but George Ogden followed him and reached out, catching him by the shoulder. 'What have you got to do with it?' snarled Ballington, but Ogden held on until PC Hebden, arrived. As he approached the carriage, someone shouted out that a man had stabbed his wife and pointing to Ballington, cried, 'That's the man who done it!' The constable at once took Ballington into custody, noticing that his captive had a superficial wound on his throat, which was bleeding slightly. Several men, including William Barratt, a railway porter, helped to carry Ellen Ballington out of the carriage and lay her down gently on the platform. Quite a crowd had now gathered and someone asked, 'Who did this?'

'Me!' answered Ballington, 'It's what I intended doing long enough. I should have done it sooner. It is the best end to it.' Amazingly, William Barratt seemed more concerned with his portering work than with the injured Ellen and as the stationmaster had now also arrived, he left to see his train to its next destination!

Seeing his wife lying on the platform, Fred Ballington bent down and attempted to kiss her. 'Goodbye,' he said. 'I have done it and it's all through eighteen pence.' The ambulance men now arrived and saw that the injured woman was bleeding from a wound in the throat, which one of the onlookers was attempting to staunch with his thumb. The woman's clothing was saturated with blood and Ernest Bamford, one of the ambulance men, found a towel and attempted to bandage the wound before placing her in the ambulance and taking her to the Royal Infirmary, where she died shortly afterwards.

The bloodstained knife was handed to PC James Lane and he noticed that the large blade appeared to have been recently sharpened. Fred Ballington, who was by now firmly secured, looked perfectly calm and sober as he was being taken away, first to have his own wound dressed and then to be handed over to the Manchester City Police by PC Hebden at Whitworth Street police station. As he was being taken to the cells, Ballington remarked, 'This is all through her not giving me eighteen pence so that I could go to Blackpool to get work and her having all that money.' On being searched, the police found that Ballington had the sum of 1s 10½d in his pocket. At 8 p.m., he was cautioned by Inspector Richard Thomas of C. Division and charged with 'the murder of Ellen Ann Ballington by stabbing her with a knife in the right cheek and below the left ear whilst in a third-class compartment' – whether the crime would have been even more heinous if it had been committed in a first class compartment is not clear!.

One of twenty meat plates made for Samuel Ballington, after be took over the business after the death of his mother. (Courtesy of Frank Ballington)

The prisoner leaned forward. 'Is she dead?' he asked and then putting his hand to his forehead, muttered, 'The sooner they hang me, the better, then I shall follow her and be with her.'

A post-mortem was performed by Dr Herbert Henry Rayner, the resident surgical officer at Manchester Royal Infirmary. He found the body to be that of a well nourished woman aged about forty, whose lips and skin were blanched from loss of blood. On the right side of the face close to the mouth, there was a lacerated wound about 4in in length and ½in in depth. On the left side of the neck below the left ear was a stab wound about ¾inch in length, which passed directly inwards for about 2½in, penetrating the internal jugular vein. This had led to severe bleeding into the surrounding tissue. There were no other signs of injury, brain and skull were normal and the cause of death was haemorrhage.

On 26 May, Fred Ballington appeared before the Manchester magistrates, looking rather unkempt, with his coat collar turned up over his unshaven face. The hearing lasted only a few minutes, during which Ballington was accused of murdering his wife and also of attempted suicide. He was then remanded in custody to await trial. A note in the file at the National Archives, from the accused man to the Clerk of the Assizes dated 24 June 1908, reads:

I wish to make an application under the Poor Prisoners Defence Act 1903. I am committed to the Assizes on the charge of wilful murder of my wife on 25 May last. As I have no means whatsoever to obtain a legal defence for my charge, I am hoping that you will endeavour to assist me.

Ballington was provided with legal assistance.

The trial began on the first day of the Manchester Assizes on Monday 25 May 1908, before Mr Justice Bucknill. Spencer Hogg and Mr Rathbone acted for the prosecution, whilst for the defence appeared Gilbert Jordan. The jury having been sworn, the accused man was allowed to be seated in the dock and in reply to the charge of murder, replied in a firm voice, 'Not Guilty' In reply to the second charge of attempted suicide, he appeared to hesitate a moment before repeating 'Not Guilty' Ballington listened intently as Spencer Hogg outlined the case for the prosecution.

The facts of the case were sordid and sad and the motive for the crime of murder seemed small and inadequate. The tragedy seemed to have been caused by his annoyance at his wife throwing him out of the family home, culminating in a feeling of revenge when she would not lend him a small amount of money. The accused's drinking habits led to rows between him and his wife and on occasions, he left the family home for a period, only to return later. Eventually, the deceased woman and her son ordered him out of the house and he went to lodge in Hulme on 3 May. On the day before the tragedy, he had appeared at the house and requested to stay the night – this had been refused and he left.

Counsel then outlined the events of 25 May, which ended with the death of Mrs Ballington after she had been savagely attacked by her husband. After Mrs Ballington had sat down in the railway carriage, the accused had joined her and once again, he had asked her for money. Upon being refused, he grabbed hold of her and said, 'We will have a kiss,' before his wife broke away. It was shortly afterwards that he assaulted her with a knife, resulting in a fatal injury to the jugular vein.

The accused man wrote a statement four days after his arrest, but there was little in it to contradict the prosecution's case. It was read out to the court, the final words being, 'She got into the carriage and then you know what happened. I did it on the spur of the moment, in a moment of mad passion.' Mr Hogg reminded the jury that although it was possible that the defence would try to make out that the blows were committed at a time when the accused was of unsound mind, his statement made it quite clear that he had intended doing it for some time.

Samuel Ballington appeared greatly distressed as he told the court of the frequent quarrels at home between his father and mother. Answering a question from the defence, he said that he knew that his father had only been working one day a week lately. He also agreed that his father had a knife similar to the one produced in court. He was followed by several other witnesses, all of whom had seen some or all of the events at the station.

When it came time for the defence, there was little that Gilbert Jordan could say in the face of the prosecution evidence. 'The motive put forward,' he told the court, 'was very small indeed' and on the subject of malice aforethought, which was an essential ingredient of murder, he invited the jury to consider that the wounds were of such a nature as not to suggest that they were done with deliberate intention and that therefore, they should bring in a verdict of manslaughter.

The jury were absent for fifteen minutes and then returned with a verdict of 'Guilty' Mr Justice Bucknill placed on his head a scrap of black material, carefully weighted at the corners to keep it in place, whilst he delivered the sentence, which he did in a state of some emotion, at one time almost breaking down. 'I do not wish to add anything to the prisoner's feelings, but from what he had said at the time of the murder, I firmly believed that the accused loved his wife.'

Ballington, now standing, heard the judge's words with a stern face and then walked slowly below to the cells.

The grave of Ellen Ann Ballington at Glossop. (Courtesy of Frank Ballington)

The death certificate of Fred Ballington. (Crown copyright)

Later, Ballington insisted that there should be no attempt at a reprieve, although the Home Secretary was approached to that effect. He declined to interfere with the course of the law and Fred Ballington was executed on Tuesday 28 July by Henry Pierrepoint, assisted by William Willis. The proceedings were carried out expeditiously and skilfully, Ballington being given a drop of 6ft 10½in. A note in Pierrepoint's hanging book said, 'Thick neck.' The scar in the accused man's throat had been reopened in the fall, but death was due to fracture of the skull and dislocation of the neck. Three weeks after the execution, Samuel William Ballington got married.

An intriguing footnote to this case is that the post-mortem report on Ellen Ballington includes the words, 'The uterus showed very early pregnancy.' Assuming that Mrs Ballington had not taken a lover, which hardly seems likely, the baby must have been conceived in the last few days of her and Fred living together. It is extremely unlikely that either Fred Ballington or his wife knew about the 'happy event' that was to be theirs in nine months time, but if they had, what a difference it might have made. Ellen Ballington was buried in Glossop cemetery, where she now lies with several of her relatives.

8

DEATH OF A SHOPKEEPER

In 1913, Yorkshire Street, Oldham, was, and still is, a bustling thoroughfare, one of the focal spots of the town. It consisted mainly of shops and commercial premises, including at No. 43, the shop belonging to fifty-four-year-old Daniel Bardsley, a dealer in books and stationery. The premises consisted of the shop, with living accommodation above, although Bardsley himself lived with his brother and sister-in-law in Egerton Street, Oldham. The rooms upstairs at the shop were used as office accommodation and storage.

Bardsley had left school at thirteen and obtained a position with Clegg's stationers, setting up on his own when Mr Clegg moved to another shop. The *Oldham Standard* described him as being closely connected with the Salem Moravian Church and the Oldham Lyceum and stated that he had been a keen supporter of local amateur dramatics. The newspaper also described him as having a happy disposition.

The business was sufficiently profitable for him to employ three full-time assistants: Annie Leach, who had worked for Bardsley for the past eleven years; Clara Hall, only recently taken on; and Edward Hilton, who at the time was working out his notice. Hilton was seventeen years old and had not long since returned from a visit to Canada. He worked for Mr Bardsley as a packer and window cleaner. Bardsley, who was inclined to be a little pernickety, expected his staff to work long hours and to keep their minds on their jobs, something that Hilton found difficult to do. Finally, after an argument with the young man about the state of the shop windows he had been set to clean, the exasperated Bardsley lost patience and gave the boy his notice. Hilton, who had become fed up anyway with the long hours he was expected to work, affected not to be bothered at his loss of employment, and took a month's notice.

Yorkshire Street, Oldham. Bardsley's shop was towards the far right. (Author's collection)

Yorkshire Street as it is today. (© A. Hayhurst)

Opinions of Hilton by the other two assistants varied. Annie Leach called him a 'bad packer' meaning that he could not do his work properly. In her evidence at the trial, she said that Hilton could not clean the shop window properly either and Mr Bardsley sometimes made him do it twice. 'I think,' she told the court rather waspishly, 'that he could have done better if he had tried.' On the other hand, her colleague, Clara Hall, said Hilton was 'A fairly good packer, a willing sort of a chap about the shop. He was not lazy or stupid.' Perhaps this differing of opinion had something to do with the varying lengths of time the two women had been working for Mr Bardsley and the difference in their ages.

On Saturday morning, 26 July, Clara Hall was sent by her employer to the premises of Hirst Bros Jeweller's, and brought back with her six gold signet rings on approval, which she duly handed over. Whether this was a personal purchase by Bardsley or whether the rings constituted part of the shop stock is not clear, but both the female assistants were aware of them and Miss Hall was adamant that Hilton had not seen them and she denied in court having told him about them.

At 10 p.m. that evening as usual, Hilton fixed the gates which were locked on to the shop front, after which no one could enter the shop from the street. This was his final duty before leaving the shop and at the same time, Annie Leach took the day's takings upstairs to her employer, as she usually did, leaving 20s in the till as a float. Mr Bardsley was busy doing his paperwork and asked Annie about the address of a boy he was writing to, to make him an offer of employment to replace Hilton. 'Is he going, then?' she asked. 'He doesn't want to and he's asked for another chance,' said Bardsley, without giving an indication one way or the other. Annie then went downstairs and she and Clara Hall left at about 10.30 p.m., using the back door into the yard, whilst Bardsley stayed behind on his own doing his books. This was his invariable habit on Saturday evenings and he rarely got home to his brother's house much before 11.45 p.m., by which time John Bardsley and his wife were usually in bed.

The premises in Yorkshire Street were looked after throughout the night by the Higher Yorkshire Street Watch, and at 1 a.m., watchman James Greaves visited the back of the premises and finding No. 43 secure, continued on his rounds. At 3 a.m., he returned again and this time he found the yard door wide open and the house door closed only with the thumb latch. Opening the door, Greaves found it obstructed and on looking in, he could just see a pair of legs on the floor and by the light of his torch, he saw that they belonged to Daniel Bardsley, who was lying on the stone floor, on his back.

Greaves looked round for a constable, but not finding one, he went along to the Central police station at the Town Hall, which was only a short distance away and told Inspector Johnson his story. The inspector immediately detailed PC Finney to follow him and the three men hurried off to Yorkshire Street. Between them, they managed to gain entrance and found the body of Daniel Bardsley lying in the passageway, his head surrounded by a pool of blood. He was quite dead and lying near to the body, on each side of the head, were a heavy Indian club, weighing over 2lb and a bloodstained dumb-bell, which was later found to be from Bardsley's shop stock. His hat was also on the floor, lying a few inches from his head. Scattered around the body were a number of keys and several letters, which Mr Bardsley had evidently been intending to post on his way home.

The dead stationer had suffered a severe beating round the head and there were several bruises. Both his hands were clenched and had blood on them, as did his clothes. There was blood on the shelves on the right-hand side of the body and also on the shop goods stored there. At the post-mortem, it was disclosed that there were also extensive fractures to the skull, which had been the cause of death. According to Dr Robert Jackson, pathologist at the Oldham Royal Infirmary, the Indian club could have caused the injuries to the head and the dumb-bell might have been responsible for a lacerated wound approximately 1½in long at the point of the chin. At least two blows must have been given and considerable force used.

A search of the premises disclosed a safe in the upstairs office that appeared to have been tampered with and a chisel was found on a shelf at the bottom of the stairs, corresponding exactly to marks on the safe, which the intruders had failed to open. The drawer of the cash register in the front of the shop was open and empty. Enquiries at the neighbouring properties failed to shed any light on the matter, no one having heard anything at all. In fact, the confectioner who lived next door to Bardsley's shop later told the police that he had known nothing about the murder until 11 a.m. on Sunday morning. At 4.15 a.m., PC Albert Finney finally removed the body to the mortuary. There, he searched the dead man's clothes, but found no money or anything of value.

At 10.15 a.m. on the Sunday morning, DC Charles Jones visited Bardsley's shop and found Edward Hilton and several other people there. Hilton claimed that he had heard about the murder and had come round to the shop to see if he could help the police. He told Jones that he had left the shop at around quarter to ten on Saturday night and he had then gone to meet a friend at Hollinwood Wakes and had stayed there until just before midnight, when he returned home. Hilton's story was not very coherent and he insisted that although he had known this 'friend' for three months, he did not know his name. He was asked to go with DC Jones to the police station at the Town Hall, where Inspector William Piggott told him that he would be detained until the police were able to verify his story.

Hilton was then lodged in the cells whilst a search was made at his home, 105 Manchester Street, Oldham, where the police took possession of his working suit and other articles, taking them back to the police station, where they showed them to Hilton, who agreed that they were his.

On examination, the garments appeared to be saturated with blood on the trouser leg and a pair of socks was similarly stained. 'Hilton,' warned Inspector Piggott, 'be careful of what you say, because you are going to be charged on suspicion of having caused the death of Daniel Wright Bardsley at 43 Yorkshire Street.' A search of Hilton's pockets disclosed 4s 1d and three foreign coins, after which he made another statement, in which he said that:

I went to the shop with another fellow, but I cannot say what his name is. I have been meeting him for the past three months. I knocked at the back door and Mr Bardsley said, 'Who is it?' I replied, 'It's me. I have come back for something.' Mr Bardsley then opened the door and we rushed him. Once he was on the floor, I said to my companion, 'That will do,' to which he replied, 'We may as well finish it.'

The police made it quite clear to Hilton that they found it difficult to believe his story of Mr Bardsley being beaten by a mysterious companion and soon, Hilton was changing his story yet again and giving the police the name and address of twenty-year-old Ernest Edward Kelly, of 119 Ward Street, less than a mile from Bardsley's shop. Hilton was taken to this address by DC Jones and on seeing Kelly, pointed and said, 'That's him.' Detective Jones began to question Kelly, who put his finger to his lips, saying 'Come into the front room and don't let my mother hear you. I will show you where I put all that I got.' Kelly then took Jones into the back yard where, from a pile of soil, he took out four gold rings, 9s 6d in silver, 1s 8½d in copper and four keys, one of which fitted the letter box at the shop. The accused men were then taken to the Town Hall, where Kelly was undressed and searched, and Jones noticed that there were blood stains on his socks and coat.

Once Kelly had disclosed the whereabouts of his share of the loot, Hilton also agreed to show where he had put his share and he took the policemen to Painter Street, where he turned down a passageway and put his hand into a hole in the

No. 119 Ward Street, Oldham, where Kelly was arrested. (© A. Hayhurst)

wall. Pulling out a handkerchief, he opened it and showed Inspector Piggott £1.5s 6d in silver, 4d in copper and two gold rings. These proved to be two of the six that had been bought by Mr Bardsley on the 26th and matched the four found at Kelly's house.

Hilton and Kelly were then charged that they feloniously and with malice aforethought, did kill and murder Daniel Wright Bardsley, to which Hilton replied, 'I never touched him with the club. I never touched him with anything. I gave him a drink of water, that's all.'

'Guilty for me.' said Kelly. 'I hit him with the club and then threw it down.' Pointing to Hilton, he went on, 'He hit him twice with the club and then ran upstairs.' Detective Jones' own statement ends, 'I have since tried the key produced [presumably one of the four taken from Kelly] and it fits the letter box of Mr Bardsley's shop door.'

At Oldham Magistrate's Court on Monday 28 July the two men were placed in the dock to face a formal charge of murder. The proceedings took only a few minutes, during which the two female shop assistants, Miss Leach and Miss Hall, wept bitterly. The Chief Constable, Mr D.H. Turner said that the motive for the crime was clearly robbery and although some of the property had been recovered, he thought that there was still more to find. Asking for the two accused to be remanded in custody for one week, he said that he would be drawing the facts of the case to the attention of the Home Secretary and that articles of clothing, particularly Hilton's, would be sent for analysis. This being granted, the two were speedily removed from the dock and returned to the cells.

The inquest on Daniel Bardsley opened in the Town Hall, members of the public not being admitted. The Chief Constable again looked after the interests of the Crown, whilst a local solicitor, Mr Nicholson, appeared for Hilton. The Coroner, Dr Carson, opened the proceedings by addressing the jury:

> The next case is that of Daniel Wright Bardsley, whose body you have viewed in the mortuary. I want you to pay special attention to this case, as the man was found dead in his own premises at 2 o'clock on Sunday morning. His head was in such a condition that it made it absolutely certain that the man had received wounds from some person or persons who had caused his death. It will be your duty to hear the evidence and if you think this sufficient, to return a verdict of murder.

John Andrew Bardsley, the brother of the dead man, was first to give evidence and said that he had known nothing about the murder until 5 o'clock on Sunday morning. His brother was in the habit of staying at the shop until very late hours and it had not occurred to the witness or his wife that there was anything amiss when Daniel had not come home by the time they went to bed.

Annie Leach was next and it was soon obvious that she was suffering from extreme emotion. She had hardly entered the witness box when she collapsed, unconscious, and was quickly carried out of the courtroom. Her place was taken by the night-watchman, James Greaves, who acquainted the court with the circumstances of his discovery of Mr Bardsley's body lying in a pool of blood. Shortly afterwards, Miss Leach re-entered the witness box, she was now more composed, although she asked to be allowed to give her evidence seated. She said that she left Mr Bardsley at around 10.30 p.m., at which time Hilton was fastening the front gates, so that no one could go in and out by the front entrance. Hilton's job, she said in a low voice, was to clean the windows, do the packing and go on errands. 'You have been working there for eleven years,' the Coroner said. 'Could he do the work properly?' The answer was an emphatic 'No.'

'He could not do it as well as you could?' asked the Coroner.

'I don't know,' was the reply. The Coroner persisted.

'Could he have done it better if he had tried?' Miss Leach tried unsuccessfully to conceal her contempt for the young man.

'Yes, but he was very stupid.'

On further questioning, she said that she had never seen the wooden club or the dumb-bell before. After being asked to point Hilton out to the court, the unfortunate woman collapsed again and her ordeal, for the time being, was over.

Clara Hall said that she had been sent by Mr Bardsley for the six rings. She did not think that Hilton had seen them and denied talking to the young man about them. Her view of the accused Hilton differed somewhat from that of her older colleague. When asked, 'What sort of a packer was Hilton,' she replied, 'Alright.'

'Would you call him lazy?'

'No.'

Detective Jones gave evidence of the finding of Mr Bardsley's body and the arrests of Hilton and Kelly and confirmed that the two were properly cautioned. DI Piggott then produced a pint pot which a witness said he had found by the body, containing water and a cloth. He also produced two wooden boxes, stained with what appeared to be blood. The boxes contained colouring crayons. At this moment, the distressed Annie Leach, now sitting in the public gallery, fainted again.

Dr Jackson gave an account of the post-mortem and agreed that the wooden club could have caused the injuries to Mr Bardsley's head. The Coroner then motioned towards the two accused and asked them if they had anything to say on their own behalf, cautioning them in the usual way. Kelly said, 'Only the club was used. The dumb-bell was not used at all. I have never seen the dumb-bell before.' Hilton remained silent. Inspector Piggott said that the club was now known to have belonged to Kelly. The coroner summed up, pointing out that the two men had been in possession of belongings known to have been on Mr Bardsley's person when the two female assistants left the shop on the Saturday night and the jury quickly returned a verdict of murder against both the accused.

The trial proper took place on Monday 24 November 1913 before Mr Justice Avory, one of the most noted criminal lawyers of the late-nineteenth and early-twentieth century. He was described as 'thin lipped, cold, utterly unemotional, silent and humourless' and was known to be relentless towards lying witnesses and brutal criminals. This gaunt, expressionless man nodded down at the crowded courtroom and the trial commenced. After the witness evidence, it was the turn of the two accused to give their stories.

First to enter the witness box was Hilton, who throughout the hearing had not appeared to be giving much attention to what was going on. He said that he had been working for Daniel Bardsley for only three weeks, which was also the length of time that he had known Kelly. After leaving the shop on the Saturday evening, he had met Kelly, who asked him if he had any money. 'No,' he said, 'not until I get my wages from Mr Bardsley.' Kelly, he said, had then said, 'Let us attack him,' to which Hilton had replied, 'No, wait till he goes home.' They went back to the shop yard and hid behind some ladders, where in the darkness they saw the two girls leaving. 'I then went into the shop for my apron,' said Hilton and Judge Avory leaned forward, glaring at him, 'What made you think of your apron?'

'I thought that after we had got the money, it would be a clue,' stuttered Hilton, plainly discomfited by the judge's interruption.

Mr McCleary, for the prosecution, asked him, 'At the time you went into the shop for your apron, had you any intention of stealing anything?'

'No sir.' 'And at that time had it been suggested that Kelly should come in the shop with you?'

'No.'

Hilton went on:

When I got into the shop, Mr Bardsley saw me and asked what I was doing. I told him I had come for my apron and he told me to get it. I heard a noise and turned round, seeing Kelly with the club in his hand.

'Where was Mr Bardsley?' asked Mr McCleary

He was lying on the floor of the packing room. I told Kelly not to hit Mr Bardsley and then he hit him on the left side of the head. I said, 'God will punish us for this' and then Kelly hit him again. Then he asked me where the safe was and I said, 'Upstairs.' We both went upstairs and I tried to open the safe with a screwdriver but Kelly said that he had the keys, which he had taken from Mr Bardsley. We tried them, but they were the wrong ones. I then heard Mr Bardsley moaning downstairs and I went to him. He was trying to get up and I went and got some water and poured it down his throat. I then got a cloth and wiped his face. Mr Bardsley started moaning again and Kelly came downstairs and told me to take the cloth and stuff it down his throat. I put the cloth over his face and then Kelly pushed it into his mouth. Kelly then went through Mr Bardsley's pockets and pulled out a handful of silver, which he put into his own pocket. Later he gave me the silver and two gold rings. Kelly then went upstairs again to try to get into the safe and whilst he was up there, I took 20s out of the till.

We do not know if Hilton had been given any guidance by his counsel, but it must have been obvious to every legal man in the court that although Hilton may have been trying to pass all the blame on to Kelly, he was also convicting himself out of his own mouth. Mr Rycroft, for Kelly, stood up and addressed Hilton, 'I understand that you throw the whole of the blame on Kelly?' Hilton replied, 'I don't blame him for anything, only for what he did.' Rycroft's tone hardened. 'When you were in the hospital at Strangeways Gaol, did you tell a man there that you had hit Mr Bardsley twice with a club?'

'No.'

'Did you say to Kelly, "Have you anything to hit him with?" And did Kelly say, "There is a club in our yard"?'

'No.'

'Did you say at the police court, "I agreed with Kelly to rob Mr Bardsley; we expected there was money in the safe upstairs".'

'Yes.'

Then it was Kelly's turn. Going into the witness box, he said that he had met Hilton, who had told him that his employer was going to sack him.

I asked why and he just said, 'I am going to have my own back on him before I have done with him.' Hilton then said he was going to rob him and I said, 'Have you anything to hit him with?' and he said, 'Yes. There's that old club in your yard.' He then said, 'Go and fetch it' and gave me sixpence for the tram fare. I got back about ten minutes later and waited with him until the girls went. Whilst we were there, Hilton gave me a mask to hide my face.

The story now varied from the one that Hilton had given to the court. Kelly claimed that they went into the shop, where they saw Mr Bardsley coming downstairs. Kelly claimed that:

I said to Hilton, 'Can you not rob him without hitting him?' and Hilton replied, 'No. He has the keys of the safe in his pocket.' When Mr Bardsley saw that we were going to hit him, he cried out and then Hilton pulled out a revolver and said, 'Hands up.' Mr Bardsley went to the gaslamp and turned it up, the better to see us. Then he turned to run and I aimed a blow at him but I only touched his jacket. He fell on his face and remained quite still. Hilton then took the club off me and hit Bardsley on the head. Mr Bardsley did not stir afterwards.

Mr McCleary intervened, 'According to your story, it was Hilton's idea that you two should break into these premises?'

'Yes.'

'And it was Hilton's idea that you should take the club to hit him with?'

'Yes.'

'You did not say anything about the revolver at the police court.'

'Mr Piggott knew about it.' (No further mention of a revolver was made and the weapon was never produced in court.)

Mr Justice Avory, c. 1931. (Author's collection)

Horace Avory began his summing up, telling the jury that where two people act together to commit felony, and violence is used and death results, then both are guilty of murder. There could have been no doubt in the minds of anyone in the court that this was exactly what the two accused men had confessed to, even though their purpose was to blame each other. The jury took only twenty-five minutes to bring in a guilty verdict, with a recommendation to mercy because of their young ages.

The judge carefully placed the square of black cloth on his head before passing sentence of death on both:

> You are young to die the degrading death which you are now by law subject to. But it lies not with me either to express any opinion or to hold out any hope to you as to the recommendation of the jury, but it will be forwarded to the proper quarter. You hurried your victim to eternity without giving him any time to make any preparation to meet his Maker. The law is more merciful to you. It gives you that time.

It is doubtful whether Mr Justice Avory's words gave any comfort to the two young men facing him.

In the eighteenth century, criminals convicted in a capital case were often hung within two days of the trial, but the modern way was to give three clear Sundays before the execution. To avoid the hangman having to travel on the third Sunday to make preparations, executions were frequently timed for any day but Monday. Meanwhile, whilst Hilton and Kelly languished in the condemned cells, considerable efforts were being made on their behalf.

Petitions were forwarded to the Home Office and in early December, it was announced that the Home Secretary had agreed to reprieve Hilton because of his age (he had just had his eighteenth birthday) and the fact that he had been mentally defective since childhood. Neither of these considerations applied to Kelly and so his sentence had to stand. This might have been good news for Hilton, but the citizens of Oldham were outraged. Kelly was now due to die on Wednesday 17 December and there was great indignation that he had not been shown the same mercy as his accomplice, who almost everyone thought had been the main culprit.

The Oldham Labour Party, representing 25,000 members, sent a resolution of protest to the Home Secretary, as did the Mayor of Oldham and the workers at Messrs. Platt Brothers, where Kelly had worked. A crowd of some 50,000 people assembled on Monday 15 December to protest against the Home Secretary's decision and large crowds collected in front of Oldham Town Hall, where the mayor made an address from the balcony through a megaphone and then moved the following resolution

> This public meeting of inhabitants of Oldham is strongly of the opinion that, inasmuch as the death sentence passed on Edward Wild Hilton, one of the prisoners found guilty of the murder of Daniel Wright Bardsley at Oldham has been respited, the same clemency ought to be extended to Ernest Edwin Kelly, the other prisoner

and earnestly hopes that the Secretary of State will be able to give effect to this recommendation.

A member of a prominent local family, Mrs Lees, waited to second the resolution, but was unable to do so because of the rowdiness of the huge crowd. She struggled valiantly with the megaphone, shouting that she would stay there all night if necessary in order to complete her task. There had been some controversy in the town over the past few days as a rumour spread round that she had used her best efforts to secure a reprieve for Hilton and had done nothing for Kelly. This she stoutly denied, telling the crowd that she had signed petitions for both the accused and she had also written to the town's two Members of Parliament and had met both Mrs Hilton and Mrs Kelly. She had also visited both the accused at Strangeways Prison. 'I regret,' she shouted, 'as much as any of you that the Home Secretary has not seen his way to reprieve both.' The resolution was then carried unanimously.

Word came on Tuesday 16 December that there would be no reprieve for Kelly and there were remarkable scenes outside the Town Hall, as a large crowd gathered. These people then marched the seven miles to Manchester and by 2 a.m. on Wednesday morning, some 8,000 people were gathered outside the prison. They were kept in some semblance of order only by a large force of policemen. Meanwhile in Oldham itself, there were more scenes of disorder, tramcars were attacked and every pane of glass in the police station was broken. Amazingly, no one was injured and the police made no arrests.

Kelly was hanged at 8 a.m. on 17 December with a huge crowd surrounding the prison. It was generally felt that if both men had been hanged, that would have been acceptable, but reprieve of only one, for whatever reason, was unfair. Little thought, it seems, was given to the innocent victim of a cruel and senseless attack.

9

DEATH IN CARRS WOOD

Northenden, 1923

Percy Sharpe was fourteen years old on 3 June 1923 and left Chester Street School, Ardwick, six weeks later, hoping to find a job as an electrician. These were few and far between and so three times a week he attended his local Labour Exchange in Queen Street, off Albert Square Manchester. When he returned, usually unsuccessful, he would carefully place his Labour Exchange attendance card on the mantelpiece and hope for better news next time he went.

Percy lived with his parents, Percy and Ellen Sharpe, at 32 South Street, Ardwick, and every week, his mother gave him 6*d* pocket money, which she said he usually spent immediately. There was nothing much to do in the streets about his home, apart from a kick-about with a few of his friends, but once a year he went to the boy's camp organised by the Chester Street Play Centre, although this year, feeling himself now grown up, he had decided not to go. Apart from that, he attended the Chancery Lane Wesleyan Sunday School every Sunday and he had not long ago spent six weeks off with rheumatic fever, from which he was now recovered.

On Tuesday 4 September 1923, at around 8 a.m., Percy said 'goodbye' to his father, who was going out to work and half an hour later, left the house himself to make another attempt to get a job. He was wearing a patched pair of trousers held up with braces, collar and tie, shirt, waistcoat, stockings and boots. He also had on his overcoat and cap. Tucked into his inside jacket pocket was his diary, which he usually carried about with him and his Labour Exchange card. Having spent his pocket money quickly, as usual, he had no money on him, which meant that he had to walk to the Labour Exchange, although Percy was used to that and thought nothing of it. There was still no good news waiting for him at the Labour Exchange and he set off on the walk home, from which he usually returned at about noon.

However, on this particular morning, he failed to appear and by two o'clock, his mother was anxiously scanning the street for a sight of him.

It was twenty-five minutes past two when James Oswald Etherington, a plate layer on the Cheadle Branch of the London, Midland & Scottish Railway was working on the down line, about 800yds distant from Northenden Junction, when suddenly, he heard a loud scream. It sounded to him as though it was a young boy, and it came from the direction of a small stand of timber, known locally as Carrs Wood. Thinking it was someone larking about, he took no notice and continued with his work. Then he heard it again and, curious, he went to look, running down the line of railway in the direction of the sound. He had gone about 600yds when he caught a glimpse of a figure in the wood. It was a man, about 5ft 10in tall, wearing a light-coloured mackintosh and a cap, who appeared to be making his way to a footpath in the Gatley direction. Quickly, the man was obscured by willow beds and he saw no more of him.

Suddenly, the screaming started again and looking round, he saw a boy on the footpath, making for the main road to Northenden, where there were steps leading up to a bridge. The boy appeared to be wearing red trousers and a white shirt and was still screaming. He climbed the steps painfully and Etherington followed him, by now beginning to get most concerned. The boy became obscured for a few seconds as a train went by and then Etherington saw that he was now leaning against a wall. He saw, with horror, that the boy was not wearing trousers at all and that the red colour he had mistaken for cloth was blood. As Etherington ran up to him, the boy said, 'A man has stabbed me. He did it with a knife.'

'What's your name, sonny?' said the plate layer.

'Percy Sharpe.'

'Where do you come from?'

'Ardwick,' said the badly injured boy.

'Did you know the man?'

'No,' was the reply. 'He is a tall man and he had a dark grey suit on and a mac and a check cap.' Etherington picked the injured boy up carefully in his arms and made for the nearby Rose Hill Hospital.

Shortly before, the signalman at Northenden signal box, James Edwards, had seen what appeared to him to be a young girl in a red skirt running down the footpath towards his cabin. 'Come quickly. I'm dying.' The voice was that of a boy. 'A man's stabbed me up yonder.' The boy sat down and leaned back against the bridge. Edwards could see a red gash on his left side, with blood oozing out. Then Etherington arrived and Edwards saw him pick the injured boy up and take him towards Rose Hill. As he went, he shouted to the signalman and told him to get help, as the boy had been stabbed.

Catherine Emmeline Eastman, a nurse at Crescent Road Hospital, Crumpsall was doing relief work at Rose Hill Opthalmic School that day and saw Etherington come in carrying the injured boy. The boy appeared to be wearing very little clothing and what little he did have on was heavily bloodstained. Etherington laid the boy down gently on a bench and the lad moaned softly and said in a whisper, 'Put me on a bed. I'm dying.' For the next five minutes, Nurse Eastman did what she could to staunch the flow of blood, putting the boy in blankets with several hot water bottles around him, during which Percy remained quite conscious and wished to talk. 'I am Percy Sharpe and I've been stabbed,' he told the nurse. 'We took a tramcar from Oxford Street to Alexandra Park and walked to Gatley.' Just then, Sergeant Edmund Ernest Furniss of the Cheshire Constabulary arrived and questioned the boy who, he noticed, had a wound in the left breast that, despite the best efforts of the nurse, was still bleeding profusely. 'How did you get the wound?' he asked.

'I was stabbed by a man in Carrs Wood. He stabbed me with a knife,' said the boy in a low voice, 'and then he wiped it on the grass and put it in his pocket.'

Considering his distressed state, the boy was able to give a surprisingly good description of his attacker to the sergeant:

> He was rather tall, clean shaven, hair turning grey, wearing a dark-grey suit with a dark tie, strong black boots, check cap and light raincoat and he came with me from Oxford Road, Manchester, having promised me some work. We came by bus about dinner time to Northenden, then walked to the woods.

By this time, it was clear that Percy Sharpe was struggling to remain conscious and the sergeant decided to go to Carrs Wood, where he met PC Jones, who showed him several articles of clothing, including a boy's overcoat, waistcoat, cap and a khaki handkerchief. The waistcoat was inside a jacket and the jacket inside the overcoat as though all three garments had been taken off at once. On the grass at his feet he saw three patches of blood as big as a penny. He then went across the field to a fence on top of a culvert and there, he said, he saw 'pots of blood'. Later the area was subjected to a search by eight police officers, but little or nothing else was found.

Meanwhile, back at the hospital, PC Sandford Bramall had arrived and did his best to question the boy and write down his answers. Percy was now totally exhausted and could only talk in spurts. At the end of the statement, the boy said, 'shut up' and lapsed into semi-consciousness. At 3.05 p.m., Dr Richard Smith Hardman arrived at Rose Hill and examined the boy. According to his report, Percy was suffering from an incised wound just below and outside the heart, about 3in long, perforating completely through the chest wall and into the pleural cavity. Blood and air were being sucked into the cavity as the boy breathed. Dr Hardman applied a sterile dressing to stop the bleeding and then gave the boy a sip of brandy. 'No more of that,' said Percy, 'I am a teetotaller!' Dr Hardman then took Percy to Stockport Infirmary in his own car and was somewhat relieved when he got there, to find that the boy was still alive. In the meantime, efforts had been made to contact Percy's parents and his father arrived at around 11 p.m., to find his son unable to speak, although he did appear to recognise his father. He continued to sit by his son's bedside until 5 a.m., when the boy died.

Stockport Infirmary, now closed, where Percy Sharpe died. (© A. Hayhurst)

A post-mortem was performed later on that day by Dr Roland Nightingale, who found several bruises and abrasions on the boy's wrists. There was a clean cut wound on the left side of the body, about 1½in in length and 3½in below the left nipple. The weapon had penetrated about 1¾in between the sixth and seventh ribs and in the doctor's opinion, the cause of death was violence which had probably been done with a large knife, something like a jack knife. There was, he said, no evidence of any sexual attack. When questioned at the Coroner's Inquest, Dr Nightingale said that the boy's attacker might well have been able to avoid any blood getting on his clothing, but might have got some on his hand.

Police enquiries proceeded and on 11 September Inspector Kingman was walking along Gatley Road in the early afternoon when he saw a man who fitted the description of the boy's attacker. He approached the man, who was sitting on a log of wood by the side of the lane. The man, who was reading a newspaper, was wearing a grey jacket and vest, khaki trousers and cap, soft linen collar, black tie and black boots. Nearby, three young boys were playing.

Kingman told the man that he was a police officer and asked him where he was on 4 September. The man, giving the name of David Colthorpe, said that he had not been to Gatley since the flower show on 1 September. 'Where were you last Tuesday, the 4th?' persisted the inspector.

'I went to the Labour Exchange in Wellington Road, Stockport and then came to Cheadle on the tram. I was at the Barnes Convalescent Home at around 5 p.m. and a policeman asked me if I had seen a strange man about and I said that I had not.'

The inspector gazed at him closely. 'You look to me as if you answer the description of the man who is wanted for the murder of the boy last Tuesday,' he said. Colthorpe pointed to the newspaper he had been reading. 'I am just reading about it in the paper,' he said. 'Are you anything to do with these boys?' said Kingman, pointing to the three lads.

'I pass my time with taking the boys out. It is a hobby of mine. I like boys.'

'Did you have any boy out with you last Tuesday?' said the by-now very suspicious officer.

'No, I had a walk around the grounds of the convalescent home.'

'Where are your mackintosh and the trousers belonging to the rest of your outfit?'

'My mackintosh is hanging up in the lodging house and the trousers are under the bed.'

'When did you change them?'

'Last Friday.' Almost as an afterthought, Inspector Kingman asked, 'Where is your knife?' He expected a negative reply, but to his surprise, Colthorpe answered, 'I gave it to Chris Peacock this morning. He lent it to me three weeks ago and asked me for it back this morning.'

Telling Colthorpe to come with him, Kingman walked to the Convalescent Home, where they saw Dr Stafford. The three men then inspected the locker belonging to Christopher Peacock, who was employed there, and the inspector took possession of a small pocket knife. After making further enquiries at the home, Inspector Kingman said that he was not satisfied with Colthorpe's story and took him to Northenden police station, where he was detained. The inspector then went with DS Critchlow of the Stockport Borough Police, to Colthorpe's lodgings at 33 Canal Street. The two men searched the room and found, stuffed under the bed, a pair of trousers which looked to be a match for Colthorpe's grey jacket and a mackintosh was handed to them by another lodger. This had a stain on the back of it, which looked as though it had been in water.

Going back to the police station, the mackintosh was shown to Colthorpe, who denied that it was his. 'Mine was a different colour and was hanging on a nail behind the door,' he explained. The inspector showed Colthorpe the trousers and pointed out two spots, one apparently caused by a whitish substance, the other looking like a spot of blood. Colthorpe made no comment.

The police had been asking for witnesses and at a subsequent line-up, when there were seventeen people present, a lady named Isabella Pearson, who claimed to have seen Colthorpe with the dead boy at 11.30 a.m., on 4 September, picked him out of the line by striking him smartly across the shoulder. Mrs Pearson said that she ran a grocery shop with her husband and often went out in a cart, selling vegetables.

On 4 September, they were in Gatley Road at 11.30 a.m., near the station and whilst there, a little boy came to her off the seat by the railway arch, and asked for a penny banana, but she told him she had none. The boy then went back to the seat where a man was sitting, a man that she identified as Colthorpe. She had since seen the body at the mortuary and identified it as Percy Sharpe. Her husband, Arthur Pearson, said that he had not taken much notice of the man, but had also identified the body of Percy Sharpe as being the young boy his wife had seen.

Elizabeth Midwinter, a widow living in Old Hall Road, Gatley, said that she remembered seeing a man with a boy, near to her home at about 12.20 p.m. on 4 September, but she did not see the man full-face, as he was sideways towards her. She also had seen the body of the dead boy but did not recognise the face, although she thought the cap and coat were like the ones worn by him. She walked up and down the line five or six times before pointing to Colthorpe, although she said that she was not certain that he was the man.

Colthorpe was taken back to the police station where he told Kingman, 'It looks black against me. I have never seen that woman before in my life, but it was a fair identification.' This somewhat ambivalent remark now convinced Inspector Kingman that Colthorpe was the man he was looking for and the suspect was taken to Withington police station and charged with the murder of Percy Sharpe. A further search of the lodging house produced a shirt, which the prisoner said he had been wearing the previous week and this, together with the other articles that had been taken from him, was handed over to Mr F. Webster, Senior Official Analyst to the Home Office, for examination. Colthorpe then made a statement, describing his whereabouts on 4 September, admitting that he had been in the vicinity of the Convalescent Hospital from about 10.30 a.m., until a policeman had spoken to him at 5 p.m., asking whether he had seen a strange man about, to which he replied 'No.'

At the Coroner's Inquest, this evidence was presented and a young boy, thirteen-year-old James Henry McLean, said that he had found a knife whilst out playing and his mother had told him that he could keep it. Later, however, having read an account of the murder in the newspapers, she took it to the police station because she had noticed some dark stains on the blade.

Rosetta Walton, the daughter of a tobacconist at Higher Hillgate, Stockport, said that Colthorpe came into her shop for some twist. She had nothing to cut it with and Colthorpe produced a knife, which she later identified. Thirteen-year-old Andrew Kelly told the inquiry that the knife found by James Mclean looked like the one he had seen Colthorpe with and he thought that the last time he had seen it was on the Sunday before the murder, when he was in Vernon Park with the accused.

The Convalescent Home seems to have been something of an open house, as several witnesses said that they had seen Colthorpe there on various occasions. He was not employed at the Home, although he was sometimes used for casual jobs and seems to have been able to come and go as he pleased, spending most of his time with the young boys there.

The ruins of Barnes Convalescent Home. (© A. Hayhurst)

The final witness at the inquest was Alfred Ernest Buxton, of Church Lane, Cheadle, who said that he was driving a pony and governess cart under the railway bridge at Gatley station at 11.40 p.m. on 4 September. He noticed a boy and a man sitting on a seat and the boy pointed to him and said, 'What a nice little turn-out.' Buxton was not able to identify the man, although he had picked somebody out of the line-up, but he now accepted that his identification was false. The man was said to have been wearing black boots, but when Colthorpe's boots were produced, Buxton was adamant that they were not the ones. When asked if he could see anyone in the court who resembled the man with the boy, he looked round and said, 'No sir, I can not.'

The Coroner, Mr J.A.K. Ferns, asked Colthorpe's defence, in the shape of Mr Macbeth, if he wished to call any witnesses. Macbeth said that as all his client's statements had been produced in evidence, he had nothing more to say and the Coroner began his summing up. He reviewed the evidence and said that it was strange that despite the exhaustive search by the police, the matching trousers had not been found. Colthorpe, he said, had made four statements, which had been corroborated by witnesses as to the times they had seen him before and after the murder, but he had not been able to explain the time between two and three o'clock. The only clues, apart from the evidence of Mrs Pearson and Mrs Midwinter were the knife and the mackintosh, which Colthorpe denied were his. He pointed out that although the deceased boy had been stabbed, there was no corresponding hole in the shirt or singlet. Although it seemed clear that the boy might well have been taken to

Gatley Station as it is today. (© A. Hayhurst)

the wood for the purpose of the commission of an unnatural offence, there was no evidence of what had happened there, because in such cases, the evidence was all circumstantial. If the jury thought that Colthorpe was the assailant, his haven of refuge could well have been the nearby Convalescent Home.

The inquest had lasted over fourteen hours and it was close to midnight when the jury came back to deliver their verdict. The foreman announced, 'We find that the deceased, Percy Sharpe, died from shock, due to being stabbed with a sharp instrument and there is not sufficient evidence against David Colthorpe and we return a verdict of wilful murder against some person or persons unknown.' At this time, inquest juries were still able to accuse an individual of being the perpetrator of the crime, although this practice has since been abandoned.

Colthorpe's face, which until now had remained a frozen mask, burst into a smile. Several of his friends, who had been sitting behind him (Colthorpe had not been placed in the dock during the hearing, but in the well of the court) shook him warmly by the hand. Outside the courthouse, the verdict was soon made known to the crowd that had gathered, and there was a burst of cheering, heard dimly inside the courtroom. Colthorpe, still in custody, was taken back to the cells and on the following morning, he appeared before Manchester Magistrates, where Mr F. Webster, for the Director of Public Prosecutions, said that as the inquest jury had come to the conclusion that Colthorpe was not guilty, he had been instructed that the Director of Public Prosecutions would offer no evidence against the accused and Colthorpe was immediately discharged.

The search for Percy Sharpe's murderer now continued and at 4.30 p.m. on 25 January 1924, PC Frank Lawrence arrested a man on a charge of molesting little boys, and took him to Moss Lane East police station. The man's name was Francis Wilson Booker and, when searched, the police found an Allotment Card, bearing his name, referring to Plot 369 at the Princess Road Allotments. Also found on the man were ten visiting cards bearing the name 'J. Simmons. Boot Repairer, 15 Morley Avenue, Wilbraham Road Estate, Fallowfield.' There were also five small notebooks.

Booker was detained and on 8 January PC Lawrence together with PC Derbyshire, went to 38 Carter Street, Chorlton-on-Medlock and spoke to Booker's landlady, Mrs Margaret Catlow. She told them that she knew Booker, who had lodged with her on two occasions and this time he had been with her for about ten or eleven months before his arrest, paying 27s a week in rent. At the time the police came, Booker had been sleeping in the bathroom (presumably because he had not enough money to pay the full rent) and before that, he had slept in the front bedroom with four other men. She showed the police officers six boxes, which she said belonged to Booker, in one of which was a small notebook. A search of the bathroom produced three pairs of boy's shorts, together with several crystal sets, which turned out to be stolen property. Going into the front cellar they found a bath, underneath which was a brown paper parcel with another pair of shorts wrapped in it. These were all taken to the police station and handed to Superintendent Tongue, who arranged for them to be examined by Mr Webster.

The constable then went to the allotments adjoining Alexandra Park and found plot 369, which included a small shed. Forcing the door, he found a wooden box full of soil, sticking out of which was the leather tab of a pair of braces. They had been wrapped in newspaper, the date of which was 25 August 1923, and PC Lawrence saw that both the braces and the newspaper had red stains on them. He also discovered a canvas wrapper, under which were nine newspapers, dated from 4 September to 23 September, although the papers from 4 September to 14 September contained no news of the Percy Sharpe case. A further search at Booker's lodgings disclosed a portmanteau which had a lock, closed by means of adjustable letters, which had to be forced off. Lawrence also found a mackintosh and a checked cap.

The boxes found at the lodgings had been examined and one contained a quantity of underclothing, a small diary and a Labour Exchange card in the name of Percy Sharpe, whose name was also written on the first page of the diary. When questioned, Booker said that he had been given the box and knew nothing about the Labour Exchange card or the diary, but his landlady said that when Booker moved from one room to another, which he seemed to have done on a regular basis, he always took that box with him. She confirmed that the mackintosh and the cap were Booker's property.

On 11 January 1924, Booker was again questioned and was shown the box and its contents. 'The note book and the labour card both bear the name of Percy Sharpe and have been identified as such by his parents,' said Superintendent Tongue, slowly. Booker stared at him, 'I found the diary on the road, the day after the murder,' he said.

The hut at plot 369. Note the box which contained the boy's braces, marked with a cross. (Courtesy of the National Archives)

'I know nothing about the labour card.' Tonge then showed him the newspapers, the pair of braces and the box of soil. 'I found the braces on the road – I don't know which one. The box belongs to me.' The Superintendent then produced the pair of trousers. 'These trousers were found wrapped in this brown paper in the cellar and they have also been identified by Sharpe's parents,' he announced. 'I found them in the parcel, with the braces, just outside Northenden,' Booker said and after hesitating went on, 'I was too frightened to take them to the police station.'

'What about these?' said Tonge, pointing to the wireless equipment. Booker agreed that they were his property, as were a pair of boots. The mackintosh and the checked cap had been stolen by him from a midden. Other pieces of clothing were produced, including a pair of grey trousers. 'Stolen off a clothes line,' Booker said.

Taking him into the charge room, the superintendent said, 'Francis Wilson Booker, I am about to charge you with a very grave offence. You are charged that you did feloniously and with malice aforethought kill one Percy Sharpe by stabbing him with a sharp implement whilst in Carrs Wood, Northenden, on the 4th of September 1923.' Booker made no reply and was then taken to the cells.

The trial, before Mr Justice Greer, commenced on 26 February 1924, with B.S. Wingate-Saul appearing for the prosecution and Kenneth Burke for the accused. Booker pleaded not guilty. The prosecution evidence ranged around the items found at the allotment and Booker's lodgings, much of which could be traced directly back to the unfortunate Percy Sharpe. Booker's rather lame reasons for having them cut little ice with the court.

Superintendent Tonge, under cross-examination, told the court that two people had been detained for this crime (meaning Colthorpe and Booker) and two others had been to the police station for questioning, but had later been released. In addition, a man named Mallinson had been a possible suspect, but he had since committed suicide. Colthorpe had been put up for identification and had been identified by Mrs Pearson. This lady had since had the chance of identifying Booker, but had failed to do so, as did her husband.

Edward Knott, a clerk with the Ministry of Labour said that Booker did not sign in on 4 September, but did so the day after. Giving his evidence, the eminent Professor John Webster said that he had examined the braces and the portions of newspaper, sent to him by Superintendent Tonge and he had identified ten brown-stained areas, which gave reactions suggestive of blood, but that the quantities were too small for him to state definitely that they were blood.

Perhaps one of the most significant pieces of evidence was a notebook belonging to the accused, in which he had listed a number of punishments that he would administer to children if they broke any of his 'Rules', such as cycling on the pavement or trespassing on the railway. Booker had no explanation for this, and no fewer than nine little boys were called to say that Booker would often accuse them of trespassing, claiming to be a policeman in plain clothes and he would then make them take their trousers down and strap them across their bottoms. However, one schoolboy, Norman Bellis, was produced by the defence, who said that he had been to Northenden with Booker several times and that the accused had never once suggested anything wrong to him.

During the course of giving evidence, Booker changed his original story and now said that he had gone into some bushes to urinate and had there found the brown paper parcel containing the braces and the clothing, which he had taken home. This did nothing for his defence except to cast doubt in the minds of the jury about anything he had said before.

Booker was found guilty, a verdict with which the judge agreed. 'The verdict of the jury,' he said, 'was in my opinion right. It was a horrible murder and there are no extenuating circumstances.' He then proceeded to pass sentence of death, to which Booker made no reply.

An appeal was launched on the grounds that the evidence was largely circumstantial and that Booker had not been identified by any of the witnesses who had been in and around Carrs Wood on the day of the crime. It was heard before the Lord Chief Justice on 4 April and after hearing submissions from prosecution and defence, Lord Hewart said, in his usual rather slow delivery, that although the evidence against the appellant was circumstantial, it was ample in quantity and convincing in character. The questions raised at the trial were questions of fact for the jury and there was no reason to interfere with their verdict. The new date for the execution was set for Tuesday 8 April and Booker was returned to his cell at Strangeways Prison to await his fate.

A report was prepared on him during the time he was in prison, which said that after leaving school, Booker had been apprenticed to a lithographic printer and had then had several jobs, found for him by his father. He had been discharged from each after a short time, either for petty theft or insolence. In 1911, he had been bound over for larceny and had been placed on probation. His father had remarried and Booker did not get on with his stepmother and he was eventually thrown out by his father for having young boys in the house in his father's absence. On one occasion, he was said to have chased his stepmother round the house with a knife and was known to have attacked a fellow employee with a hammer. He was described as morose and having a violent temper, although there was no medical history of insanity in the family. It was also mentioned that during the First World War, Booker had been awarded the Military Medal, a distinguished award, not given lightly.

On the morning of 8 April, Booker arose early and drank a cup of tea, having refused breakfast. He seemed calm and composed and greeted the chaplain when he entered the cell to give him some comfort. Quietly, the two men prayed until they were interrupted by the entrance of the executioner, William Willis, and his assistant Robert Baxter, both experienced men; Willis had hanged Freddie Bywaters the year before, whilst John Ellis had attended to his lover, Edith Thompson. Baxter was only acting as assistant executioner this time, but was to take his place as a 'Number One' later in the year.

Booker stood up, thanked the warders who had been watching over him and submitted to the pinioning of his arms. He faced death squarely and the report said that death was instantaneous. Several hundred people waited outside Strangeways Prison and women dressed in shawls were said to have had tears in their eyes, although the general opinion was that Booker deserved his fate.

At the inquest, the governor of the prison, Maj. H.E. FitzClarence stoutly refused to tell the Coroner whether or not Booker had confessed before his execution. 'I have no authority to divulge any confession or otherwise made by this man,' he said.

10

'HELLO TISH'

Thirty-six-year-old Eliza Wood called at 58 Union Street West, Oldham, every day, where her mother, Mrs Clerk, took in boarders. Naturally, she got to know the boarders well and was on friendly terms with all of them, especially James Henry Corbitt, aged thirty-seven, who had been at No. 58 for several months. Soon, they were going out together, mostly to local pubs in the evenings, when Eliza could get time off.

Corbitt was a thin, rather mournful looking man, but with a good sense of humour, who found it easy to make friends. He also had a good singing voice and used to liven the atmosphere in the local pubs by singing ballads. When he did so, he would look Eliza straight in the eyes and sing to her as if she were the only person in the room. She talked little on these occasions and sometimes had a faraway look in her eye as her boyfriend serenaded her. Not a very attractive woman, with wide-set eyes and a small, stubby nose, she wore a wedding ring, although few people ever heard her mention her husband, from whom she was separated.

Towards the middle of July 1950, Eliza was living full-time at the boarding house, standing in for her mother who was away on an extended holiday. One Thursday evening, at about 8 p.m., Corbitt was seen going out on his own by one of the boarders, twenty-two-year-old Anne Barrett, who worked in one of the local cotton mills. She thought nothing about the incident but also noticed that Eliza went out a few minutes later. Miss Barrett went to bed about midnight and sometime between one and two o'clock, she heard Corbitt return and go into his own room.

About 4 a.m., she heard Eliza come into the house by the front door and go into the kitchen, but hearing nothing further, she dozed off again. At 7 a.m., she woke up and went down into the kitchen, where she found Eliza sitting in a chair with a white cloth on her head. Anne saw that there was blood all over her clothing. 'Whatever have you been doing,' she gasped and gently lifted the cloth from Eliza's head. What she saw made her feel faint: there were two cuts on the back of her friend's head, which were bleeding heavily. At Eliza's request, she poured some cold water over the wounds, after which Eliza promptly passed out, although she soon recovered, much to Anne's relief.

After making sure that Eliza was as comfortable as possible, Anne went back to her room to get ready for work, leaving her in the care of another boarder, Mary Chorley. Eliza had knocked on Mary's door at about 5 o'clock that morning, seeking assistance, her face smeared with blood. The two women had had a short conversation whilst Mary bathed the back of Eliza's head, then Eliza had gone downstairs to the kitchen. About 6.30 a.m., Mary saw James Corbitt when he got up to get ready for work and asked him why he had attacked Mrs Wood. He admitted that he had done so and when she asked him why, he said, 'I don't know really what came over me. I am sorry that I have done it. I was jealous.'

When Anne Barrett got back, at around 6 p.m., she saw Eliza still in the kitchen, and thought that she did not look a great deal better. Some time later the same evening, Corbitt came in and she asked what had been the trouble the night before. 'I will have to tell you on the quiet,' he said and then proceeded to eat his evening meal. Shortly after he had finished, he beckoned to her and whispered to her to come up to his room, to darn a sock for him. Anne was slightly dubious about this, but there were several people in the house and she did not think that she was in any danger, so she followed him upstairs. She was hardly inside the room when Corbitt closed the door hurriedly and said, 'I want to tell you what happened.' Anne listened quietly as he told her that he was in love with Eliza, but believed she was two-timing him with another lodger, named Tommy. He admitted that he was jealous of Eliza and muttered that if he could not have her, the other man wouldn't and that he would 'finish her off.' Corbitt admitted that he had battered Eliza over the head the night before and said that when he left her, he had thought that she was dead.

'Don't be silly,' said Anne, who in reality did not know quite what to say to the obviously distressed man in front of her. 'Perhaps the best thing you could do would be to leave the house,' she told him. 'Go and get lodgings somewhere else and forget about Eliza, if she's causing you so much pain.' Corbitt made no reply and Anne left the room, feeling relieved to get away from him. A few days later, she noticed that Corbitt and Eliza now appeared to be going out again and their relationship seemed to be back on good terms.

On Saturday evening, 19 August, Alfred Egan, the landlord of the Prince of Wales Hotel, Ashton-under-Lyne, was busily serving customers, when a man (Corbitt) walked into the bar and asked for a room for the night for his wife and himself. Egan, who was struggling to cope with the rush of Saturday night drinkers, hurriedly said that the man could have room No. 7 and looking round, asked where the man's wife was. 'She will be coming along later,' Corbitt said and accepted the room key that Egan handed to him, before disappearing outside.

At half past eleven, Corbitt came back, this time accompanied by Eliza and both appeared to have been drinking. In fact, the woman appeared to be very much the worse for wear, stumbling as she walked and waving to people in the bar. 'Take no notice,' said Corbitt to the landlord, 'she's had a drink or two.'

Shortly after midnight, the pub having closed, the landlord was engaged in tidying up for the night, when he heard a succession of thumps coming from upstairs. There were eight or ten of them and Egan went upstairs and knocked on the door of room No. 7. Through the door, he asked, 'Is everything alright?' and a man's voice answered, 'We've just fallen out of bed.'

'Alright,' said the landlord, 'but please try to make less noise, there are other people sleeping, you know.'

Egan was still in the bar at 1.15 a.m. when he saw Corbitt come downstairs, clad just in trousers and shirt. He appeared to be looking for the side entrance and Egan said to him, 'the toilet's upstairs,' at which the man turned round and went back upstairs. At 2.15 a.m., he came downstairs again and seeing the landlord still cleaning up the bar, he turned on his heel and retreated once more.

The following morning the cleaner, Margaret Bailey, arrived early and started her work. Stopping to make a cup of tea, she saw a man at the bottom of the stairs, fully dressed, who nodded to her and told her that he was a resident in the hotel with his wife and asked the time of breakfast. The cleaner told him that he could have it at once, if he so wished, but the man replied, 'I don't want it now. I'm going for a walk until half past eight.'

'Well, I'll take your wife up a cup of tea if you like,' she said. The man shook his head. 'You needn't bother. I will do it when I come back.' Having said this, he went out into the street.

Disregarding his remarks, the cleaner decided that she would take a cup of tea up anyway and a few minutes later, knocked on the door of room No. 7. There was no reply to the knock, so, carefully balancing the cup and saucer in one hand, she used the other to open the door. Everything seemed to be in order, the room was in semi-darkness with the curtains drawn over the only window and in the right-hand single bed, she could see a woman, who appeared to be fast asleep, lying on her back, the blankets pulled up tight round her neck. Advancing into the room, Margaret Bailey tiptoed forward and placed the cup and saucer onto a small bedside cabinet, which stood between the two beds. Thrown casually on the bed was a woman's coat and on the floor, a pair of woman's shoes. On the other bed, which appeared to have been pulled away slightly from the wall, was a folded eiderdown at the foot, on which lay a woman's underclothes. Plainly, she thought, the couple had come back from their night out and had just flopped into bed, leaving their clothes around. Not wishing to disturb the woman, she turned round and tiptoed out again, closing the door behind her.

Coming downstairs into the bar, she met the landlord and mentioned to him that she had seen the man go out through the side entrance of the pub and so far as she knew, he had not returned. She also mentioned that his wife appeared to be fast asleep in bed. The thought passed through Alfred Egan's mind that Corbitt had gone off with the intention of not paying for his night's lodging and told the cleaner to go back up to room No. 7 and wake the woman.

Doing as she was told, Margaret Bailey climbed the stairs, knocked briefly on the door and went in. The woman appeared to be still asleep, not having stirred from the position she had last seen her in and the cleaner bent over the bed and shook the woman's right shoulder gently. Some inner feeling told her that things were not what they seemed and she pulled the bedclothes away from the woman's shoulders, revealing her naked body. In the dim light filtering through the curtains, she could see the letters WHORE written on the woman's forehead with a ballpoint pen. Realisation flooded into her brain and she stepped back hurriedly, turned and ran out of the room down the stairs and into the bar. White faced, she stammered at the landlord, 'Mr Egan. That woman in No. 7. I think she's dead!'

The startled Egan ran up the stairs to room No. 7 and switched on the light at the door, opened the curtains and then turned to the right-hand bed. The woman's body was still, although it felt warm and the skin on her face looked slightly bluish. 'God almighty,' he muttered to himself and rushed out of the room, leaving the door open. Picking up the telephone in the bar, he hastily dialled 999 and at 8.40 a.m., Sergeant Arthur Bradley of the Lancashire Constabulary arrived and went straight up to room No. 7. Having satisfied himself that the woman was indeed dead, he took stock of the room. It was quite small and sparsely furnished. Apart from the two beds and the cabinet, there was only a small dressing table and a wardrobe. On the wall to the left of the door was a fireplace, which had been bricked up, and fastened to the wall was a hand basin, with a mirror above it. On the mantelpiece lay a brooch, some beads, a woman's earrings and a hair pin and thrown untidily into the hearth he could see used matches and some cigarette ends. A shabby carpet covered the middle of the floor and on the bedside cabinet were a cup and saucer containing tea and an ash tray with five cigarette ends and a spent match. A woman's red plastic handbag lay on the cabinet. Turning back to the dead woman, he noticed the letters scrawled about an inch long on her forehead.

Hastily scribbling a few words in his notebook, Sergeant Bradley left the room, closing the door behind him. Something on the floor outside caught his eye and he bent down and retrieved a bead, which looked as though it was a match for the string on the mantelpiece. Carefully, he put it into his uniform pocket and fastened it again. At 9 a.m., DI Whittingham, stationed at Ashton-under-Lyne appeared, followed at 10 a.m., by DC William Dodding, who was also the official police photographer. He proceeded to set up his camera in room No. 7 and to take several photographs, concentrating mainly on the bed area. Later the same day, he went to the mortuary at Ashton-under-Lyne Town Hall and took three further photographs. He was to visit the mortuary again on 24 August to take three more pictures of the body, after the post-mortem.

Later in the day of 20 August, DCI Colin Campbell, head of the Fingerprint Bureau at Lancashire Police Headquarters at Hutton, arrived. Campbell was an experienced

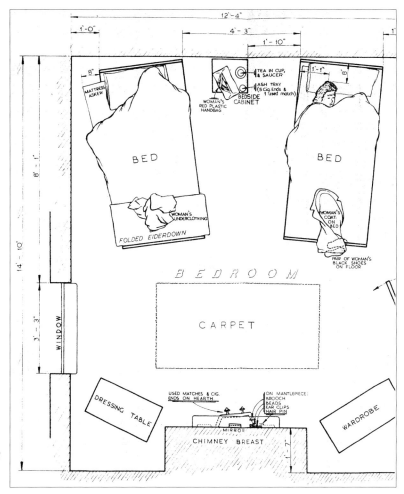

Police plan of the bedroom at the Prince of Wales Hotel, Ashton-Under-Lyne. (Courtesy of the National Archives)

officer and had been exclusively engaged in fingerprint identification for the past fourteen years. Unpacking his equipment, he found palm prints on the head of the twin bed on which the body lay and on the head and foot of the bed opposite.

At 12.30 p.m., Dr Walter Henry Grace arrived to examine the body. Dr Grace was a lecturer in forensic medicine at Liverpool University and Home Office Pathologist for the North Western region. His report, now at the National Archives, commented:

> I went into a bedroom containing two beds, on one of which was the body of a woman. The woman was dead and unclothed ... later I carried out a post-mortem examination in the presence of Detective Constable Decker. The word 'whore' was written on the woman's forehead in large letters. Her face was slightly cyanosed and slightly blue in colour. There were marks of violence on the neck, mostly at the front, consisting largely of bruises, friction marks due to the pressure of beads and another friction mark due to the application of a thin ligature to the neck. There were bruises on the inside of the

upper part of both arms consistent with some sort of struggle, where the arms had been firmly gripped. I would say that the joint between the right cornu (a bony protuberance that resembles a horn) and the body of the hyoid bone had become disrupted. This was due to manual pressure on the hyoid bone... There was a slight smell of alcohol. The beads shown to me (found on the mantelpiece) could have caused the friction marks on the front of the neck. Death was due to manual strangulation. I removed the skin of the forehead on which the word was written and handed it to Mr Thompson of the Forensic Science Laboratory.

In his report, Allan Thompson of the North Western Forensic Science Laboratory at Preston said:

I went to the Prince of Wales Hotel, Ashton-under-Lyne and in bedroom 7 saw the body of a woman. I took possession of certain objects, including Exhibit 9 (the beads), which I found on the mantelpiece. I found two more beads under the bed and two on the bed sheet. I was present when Dr Grace carried out a post-mortem. I received from him a piece of flesh from the woman's forehead containing printed marks. On 22 August 1950, I received certain objects from Detective Inspector Whittingham, including a biro pen. On 24 August, I received four pieces of black shoe lace from D.I. Whittingham. I found that three of the pieces were the same type of shoe lace and the fourth was different. I cannot say that the three pieces were originally one lace. On the flesh from the forehead was the word 'Whore.' It was done with some kind of pen and on comparing the ink with that in the biro, I found both of them to be the same type of ink.

Corbitt, of course, had not returned to the Price of Wales, but from documents found in the dead woman's handbag and conversations with the staff at the boarding house, it did not take the police long to trace him to 212 Portland Street, where it was later found out that he had been living since 22 July. Sergeant Bradley arrived at the house at 8.29 on Sunday morning and found Corbitt lying on his bed. He readily admitted his name and was then taken down to the police station. His landlady, Martha Ann Shaw, told the police that on the previous day, Corbitt had told her that he was expecting his wife and asked if she could stay. Mrs Shaw, not a woman to allow unseemly 'goings on' on her premises, refused and Corbitt left the house after tea that night and did not come home until the following day, when the police found him. She asked him if he had been out all night and he replied, 'Yes, I have.'

At 9.30 a.m., on Monday 21 August, Corbitt was interviewed at the county police office, Ashton-under-Lyne, by DI Whittingham, who told him that he was investigating the case of a woman who had been found murdered at the Prince of Wales Hotel. The woman had been identified as Eliza Wood, with whom, the inspector said, 'I have reason to believe you have been associating.'

Corbitt was then cautioned and for a few moments made no reply. Then he said suddenly:

I don't know why I did it. She started shouting and I got her by the throat. We struggled and fell off the bed on to the floor and I tied a boot lace round her neck to finish her. Afterwards, I lifted her on the bed. I cut the lace up and threw it away as I was walking home.

These had been found on the road between the Prince of Wales Hotel and Portland Street, after a police search.

Whittingham said, 'Who printed the word "Whore" on her forehead?' Corbitt replied, 'I did it with this,' producing a biro pen from his jacket pocket, together with a pen knife. 'I can write a long story about it all,' he said, mournfully. He then proceeded to make a written statement. At 2.20 p.m. the same day, Corbitt was formally charged with the murder of Eliza Wood and Corbitt wrote on the statement sheet, 'I have nothing to say at present.' When searched, a small diary was found in his pocket, which appeared to be in the same handwriting as his statement. On 21 August, Corbitt took his place in an identification line-up, when the landlord of the Prince of Wales failed to pick him out, although the cleaner, Margaret Bailey, had no hesitation in pointing to him.

After a preliminary hearing at Ashton-under-Lyne Magistrate's Court, Corbitt's trial began on 6 November 1950 at St George's Hall, Liverpool, in front of Mr Justice George Justin Lynskey. Liverpool born and of Irish extraction, Lynskey had been called to the bar in 1920 and had been in the public eye for many years, hearing the appeal of William Joyce ('Lord Haw-Haw') with Lord Chief Justice Humphreys in October 1945. He was not one for witty asides and was known to have strong views about violent crime. Appearing for the prosecution was Edward Wool KC and Corbitt was defended by Mr E. Rowson KC.

No. 212 Portland Street, Ashton-Under-Lyne, where Corbitt lodged just before the murder. (© A. Hayhurst)

Corbitt looked dapper in a dark double-breasted suit and bow-tie as he entered the dock and pleaded 'Not Guilty' in a firm voice. Mr Wool opened the trial by telling the jury that:

A morbid, squalid and repugnant tragedy took place at the Prince of Wales Hotel, Ashton-under-Lyne in the early morning of August 20. The jury will have no anxiety as to the identity of the killer or the cause of death. The accused, James Henry Corbitt, is thirty-seven and was living apart from his wife and four children and the victim, Mrs Eliza Wood, who had two children, aged eight and three, was living apart from her husband. For nine months, the accused had been living at Mrs Wood's mother's house, but in July, he left those lodgings and took others in Portland Street, where he stayed for about a month before the tragedy. When Corbitt was arrested and searched, a diary was found on him, whose entries terminated the day before the woman died.

Mr Wool then read out several extracts from the small pocket diary, on the first page of which Corbitt had written his name, National Registration number and National Insurance number. It was a diary for the current year and there was an entry for almost every date. On 20 January the entry said, 'Having got a new job, decided I would never see Liza again,' but the entry for the 27 January said, 'Made it up with Liza. Had a good night and was intimate.' The entry for 5 February said, 'For no reason whatever, was very depressed all day.' On 21 February, Corbitt had written, rather disturbingly, 'Was drunk last night. Liza told me that after being intimate with her, I nearly strangled her.'

Similar entries told the story of an up-and-down relationship between the two and it seemed clear that Corbitt's state of mind teetered between elation and depression quite often. The 31 March entry said, 'Mind is a blank today. Mental strain. Impossible to think.' The entries then appeared to get more light-hearted and by mid-June 1950, he and Liza were seeing each other on a regular basis and words like 'Lovely night' and 'Smashing' were appearing in the entries. Suddenly, on 3 July, the entry read 'Had a row with Liza about her keep telling lies. Told her I had finished with her.' Ten days later, the entry said, 'Had a hectic night. A miracle saved her.'

The relationship staggered on, and there were further rows, although they always seemed to make up quickly afterwards but by the end of July, doubts were creeping into Corbitt's mind again. The entry for Saturday 5 August included, 'We were intimate in bed. She wishes she was my wife,' but by the 12th, he was writing, 'Booked a room for Liza and I tonight. She should have met me at 5.30 but did not turn up. I will finish with her.' On 17 August, he wrote, 'Praying for one more chance to get Liza in a position to finish her off. Have lost four opportunities.' Mr Wool told the jury that these entries showed what the law called, 'Expressed malice.'

Dealing with the day of the tragedy, Wool described the couple's visit to the Prince of Wales Hotel, stressing the 'bumps in the night' in the early morning and Corbitt's leaving the hotel, with his girlfriend dead in their room:

A singularly repulsive feature was that there was a word printed in large letters on her forehead. Corbitt was asked about the man named 'Tommy' and he protested that Liza had first told him that the man was her brother and later her cousin, but he had discovered that he was no relation at all. On one occasion, after a night out, he had taken Liza back home and after knocking, found the door opened by 'Tommy,' after which there was a fight, Tommy getting the worst of it.

Corbitt's written statement was read out to the court, including that Eliza often remarked that if she saw him with another woman, she would gas herself. On other occasions, she had asked him to kill her, as she was extremely jealous of him. Corbitt claimed to the police that he could remember little of the fatal night's events, because he had drunk too much but during intercourse, Liza had shouted out, 'I want Tommy' and he had strangled her, tying the shoe lace round her throat. The statement ended, 'I must have been temporarily insane at the time, as I could not have done this thing if I had been sane.'

At the end of the prosecution case, Mr Rowson, for Corbitt, announced that he would be calling no witnesses, neither would his client be going into the witness box. 'It was plain that Corbitt and Mrs Wood had been quarrelling,' he told the jury. 'Drinking together, quarrelling, then making love and occasionally acting like beasts.' In view of the diary evidence of Corbitt's mood swings, he was asking the jury to bring in a verdict of 'Guilty, but insane.'

'Having heard the diary entries, members of the jury, could such a man know that what he was doing was morally and legally wrong?' Rowson asked.

The jury were away for fifteen minutes, before returning with a verdict of 'Guilty.' No mention was made as to Corbitt's state of mind and the judge passed sentence of death.

A report on Corbitt's mental state was prepared by Mr Cormack, Principal Medical Officer at the prison, and described Corbitt as claiming that he had indulged in orgies with his girlfriend and was suddenly overcome with the desire to kill her on their last evening together, although he had been planning it for some months.

There was no appeal and at 8 o'clock on the morning of Tuesday 28 November, he faced Albert Pierrepoint and his assistant, Harry Allen. Pierrepoint was at that time the landlord of the appropriately named 'Help the Poor Struggler' at Hollinwood, between Oldham and Manchester, and in his memoirs, *Executioner Pierrepoint*, he recounts the story of Corbitt and his lady friend frequently visiting his pub, where Corbitt would often sing. He and Pierrepoint developed a small routine when they first saw one another. Corbitt would say, 'Hello Tosh' and Pierrepoint would reply 'Hello Tish,' after a radio catch phrase of the time. Pierrepoint's book seems to indicate that Corbitt and Eliza were in his pub on the fatal night of 20 August, but Corbitt's own account of their pub visits on that evening makes no mention of the 'Help the Poor Struggler.' In view of later happenings, we can perhaps allow that this was 'journalistic license' by the hangman.

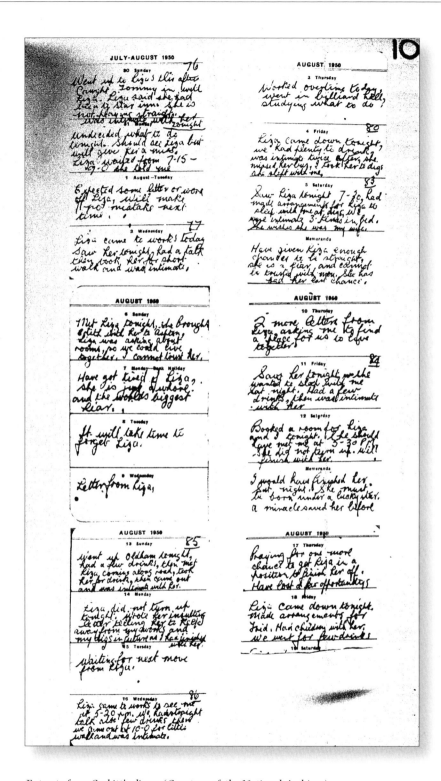

Extracts from Corbitt's diary. (Courtesy of the National Archives)

The holding cell underneath the dock at St George's Hall, Liverpool, where Corbitt awaited trial. (© A. Hayhurst)

On the day of the execution, Pierrepoint was told by the Governor of Strangeways Prison that the condemned man had made a special request that morning. Corbitt claimed that he knew the executioner and said it would help him if, when he came into the cell, he would say, 'Hello Tish,' to which Corbitt would make the usual reply.

Pierrepoint did not know the man by name, but immediately recognised him on entering the condemned cell. Anxious that everything should go smoothly, the executioner extended a hand and the two men went through their little routine, after which Corbitt was quickly pinioned and taken to the scaffold. 'Come on, Tish, old chap,' Pierrepoint said to him and the condemned man almost ran on to the scaffold and was dead within seconds.

An interesting point arose when Pierrepoint gave a series of interviews about his position of executioner to the *Empire News*. The Prison Commissioners were much exercised by this, as in accordance with usual practice, Pierrepoint had signed the Official Secrets Act, which forbade such things. In a letter from the Attorney General to the Rt Hon. Maj. Gwilym Lloyd-George MP, dated 18 April 1956, now in the National Archives, he stated that Pierrepoint's account of the execution of John Reginald Halliday Christie, the notorious serial killer, had been shown to two men who were also present at the execution and they had assured him that Pierrepoint's account was untrue. He went on to say that the executioner's account of the hanging of Ruth Ellis was likewise denied by those who were present. The Commissioners got out from under an embarrassing problem by deciding that although Pierrepoint could certainly be prosecuted under the Act for communicating facts, the Act did not forbid the communication of fiction!

11

MURDER ON IMPULSE

Tyldesley, 1951

It was Wakes Week in Tyldesley and the amusement fair was paying its annual visit to Shakerley Common. All the usual attractions were there: dodgems, swing boats, ghost train, the whip and, of course, the candyfloss and black pea stalls, which were always well patronised by the local mining community. On the early morning of 8 April 1951, Frederick Broad, a colliery engine winder, had finished work at 5.58 a.m. and was walking along the path by the side of the engine house at Wharton Hall Colliery, Atherton, and made to cross the spare ground in front of it. When he was half way across, he saw the body of a woman in a green, patterned dress, covered in a light grey coat, beneath which were protruding her stockinged legs. He bent down and spoke to the woman, but made no attempt to remove the coat. Getting no reply, he went to Atherton police station and reported the matter to PC Eric Graham.

After talking to his superiors, Graham hurried to Wharton Hall colliery where he examined the body, trying to avoid moving it as he did so. Pulling back the corner of the coat that was covering the girl's head he saw a twisted white silk scarf tied tightly round her neck. The girl was on her back, arms and legs akimbo, although so far as Graham could see, she was fully clothed. By the side of the body, he found a woman's handbag that had little in it and no money.

It did not take the police long to discover that the dead girl was twenty-eight-year-old Mona Mather, who lived locally in Little Hulton. On the previous evening, Mona had been in the George and Dragon Hotel, Elliott Street, Tyldesley, with her brother Joseph Mather and his wife. They had spent a convivial evening together and stayed until ten thirty when Joseph and his wife got up to go home, leaving Mona in the lobby of the hotel. Although she had less than 3s in her pocket, Mona was determined to go to the Wakes Fair and even if she could not afford to go on many of the rides, she could at least soak up the atmosphere and there would almost certainly be some of her friends there.

She was standing in the doorway of the hotel when a man she knew called out to her; it was thirty-one-year-old Jack Wright. He was small and thick set with a rather florid complexion and worked as a haulage hand at the Astley Green colliery. Single, he lived with his mother and step father at 3 John Street, Tyldesley. Wright was keen to go to the Wakes Fair and as Mona had known him for some time, she readily agreed to go with him.

By 11 p.m., they were enjoying the delights of the fair together and were seen by several of Mona's friends. At 11.45 p.m., they were still together and just getting off one of the rides, when Wright spotted one of his pals, Matthew Weir. Weir spoke to him, 'Hello Jackie, how are you getting on?'

'Alright,' said his friend.

'I didn't know you had started courting,' laughed Weir. Wright shook his head. 'It's one I've picked up,' he said and then, wrapping his arm round the girl's waist, the two of them disappeared into the crowd.

Police investigations led them to John Street, where Wright's step-father said that he had last seen his step-son at 11.45 a.m. on 7 April, when he went out wearing a brown pin-striped suit. An all-points bulletin was now issued for the arrest of Jack Wright and at 12.20 a.m. on Monday 9 April, an eagle-eyed DC Horace Hart, of the British Transport Police, was on duty at London Road railway station when he

John Street, Tyldesley, where Wright lived at No. 3 John Street, Tyldesley, where Wright lived at No. 3. (© A. Hayhurst)

The George and Dragon Hotel, Tyldesley, from where Mona Mather set off on her last walk. (© A. Hayhurst)

saw, coming out of the refreshment room, a man who fitted the description of the wanted man.

Stopping him, he asked the man his name. The man was inclined to be truculent and said, 'Why should I?'

'We'll have less of that,' said Hart, 'I now require to see your Identity Card.'

'Not got it with me,' said Wright. Seeing that the man might be troublesome, Hart wasted no more time. 'I have reason to believe that you are Jack Wright of Tyldesley, wanted for interview by the Lancashire Police in connection with the death of Mona Mather, of Little Hulton.'

'That's me,' said Wright and gave no more trouble as he was taken into custody. Arriving at the police office, Wright said to the policeman, 'I was with two women during the night and one did come from Little Hulton. I don't know her name and it was late when I left her to walk home on her own.' He freely admitted that he had been at the fair with the dead girl.

At 1 a.m., Wright was seen by DCs Holmes and Graham, of the Lancashire Constabulary. 'We are going to take you back to Tyldesley,' Holmes told Wright, 'Where you will be seen by one of my superior officers in connection with the death of Mona Mather, whose body was found in the early hours of Sunday morning near to Wharton Hall Colliery.' Wright merely replied, 'I don't know what's happened,' and relapsed into silence. On the way to Tyldesley police station, Wright turned to D.C. Holmes and said, 'Am I supposed to have done this job?'

'Sorry,' said Holmes. 'I can't discuss this with you now, but you'll have an opportunity to ask questions when we get to the station.' Throughout all this time, Holmes was struck by the way that his prisoner seemed totally unconcerned.

At 2.30 a.m., DCI Robert McCartney interviewed Wright, in the presence of the arresting officers. He explained who they were and said to the prisoner, 'Are you Jack Wright, of 3 John Street, Tyldesley?' Wright nodded. 'That's me,' he said.

'I expect,' said McCartney, 'that you know why you have been brought here?'

'I suppose it's something to do with a woman who's been found dead, isn't it?' Wright said.

'You have been brought here to be questioned about your movements on Saturday night and Sunday and the reason I am going to ask you these questions is because the body of a young woman was found near to Wharton Hall Colliery early on Sunday morning.'

Wright responded, 'Yes. I knew her, but I didn't know her name until that Detective,' he pointed at Holmes, 'told me tonight.' McCartney leaned forward and went on, 'Do I understand you to mean that you know the woman who has been found dead?'

Wright nodded. 'Yes, like I say, I know her, but I didn't know her name.' There was a silence and then Wright said, 'I suppose you know I was on the Wakes with her last night?'

'Well,' said McCartney, 'can you explain to me how it is that you knew the woman you had been on the Wakes with is the woman who has been found dead?' There was another silence, this time a long one, before Wright said, 'Well, here it is. It's done and it can't be helped now. I had power to prevent it if I'd wanted to prevent it, like I did once before. You can't blame her, I had nothing against her, but I'd made up my mind to have a go at her and that's all there is to it.' McCartney stopped him and read out the caution before gesturing to him to continue. 'That's alright,' said Wright, 'It's no use wrapping it up. What's done can't be undone.'

McCartney picked up a pen. 'You can either write a statement yourself or you may dictate it to me in the presence of these officers and I will record it for you,' he said.

'You put it down,' said Wright and when he had finished, the statement was read over to him and he signed it.

DC Graham then took possession of the accused man's clothing and DCI McCartney took scrapings from his finger nails. At 4.15 a.m., Wright was charged with the murder of Mona Mather and in reply to the charge, he said, 'That's correct.' Like his colleague, McCartney had also noticed that throughout, Wright appeared to be completely unconcerned at the difficult position, in which he now found himself. The due process of law followed and Wright appeared before Leigh Magistrates on 1 May 1951, where he pleaded 'Not Guilty' and reserved his defence. He was then taken to Strangeways Prison to await trial at Liverpool Assizes and lodged in the prison hospital.

Whilst in prison, Wright was interviewed by George Cormac, the Principal Medical Officer of the prison, who reported that Wright had had an elementary education, leaving school at the age of fourteen, when in the top class. Thereafter, he had had several jobs and in September 1938, he joined the Royal Navy, serving only until February 1939, when he was discharged as being unsuitable, although his character was assessed as 'Good'. After which, he had a number of jobs at local collieries, but in June 1942, he was sentenced to six months' imprisonment for four counts of larceny. When arrested, Wright resisted and had threatened the arresting officers with a large bacon knife. At the expiration of his sentence, he rejoined the colliery but on 17 December he joined the armed forces, serving mostly in India, and was demobbed in December 1945. Again, his character was assessed as 'Good' and he was noted as being a quiet, reserved type who discharged his duties conscientiously. This, despite the fact that he had been AWOL three times during his service. Since demob, he had again been working in the local collieries.

In accordance with normal practice, Wright was closely watched during his stay in prison and seemed to have settled in quickly, being clean and tidy in his habits and submitting easily to prison discipline. He passed the time with other prisoners and in the words of Dr Cormac, he seemed, 'mildly indifferent to his position and expressed no remorse or regrets, but manifested normal emotional reactions in all other fields.' This aspect of his behaviour was discussed with Wright, who told the doctor that he was a fatalist and was prepared to accept the consequences of his actions.

Dr Cormac's report also said that Wright insisted that he met Mona Mather at the pub by chance and that she had come straight towards him, making him think that she was a willing partner. Her behaviour later, whilst they were at the fair, appeared to him to confirm this view and he was convinced that they would have intercourse before the night was out. He claimed to know something of the girl's reputation and understood that she was promiscuous.

It seems that Wright was wrong about this, because he later admitted that he had made advances to the girl, but had been rebuffed, the girl telling him, 'She wasn't like that.' It was then that he had attempted manual strangulation. Wright also told the doctor that for the past ten years, he had had an idea that he would murder a woman and said that the idea came into his head to murder Mona during the time he was in the public house on the night in question, although he was later to deny this and say that he first thought about it when they were at the fair. He went on to claim that if Mona had consented to intercourse, the matter would have ended there and the murder would not have happened.

He then admitted to Dr Cormac that he had attacked women on three other occasions: the first in 1940 during the black-out, when he had grabbed a woman by the throat, but hearing someone coming, he had left her. The second occasion was of a similar nature and on both occasions, he was under the influence of drink. The third occasion was in 1947, when he was out with a married woman and his sexual advances were repulsed. Later, the doctor passed this information on to the police, who made exhaustive enquiries, but no such attacks appeared to have been reported. Cormac was of the opinion that the accused man showed no sign of mental disease and that there was nothing to indicate any perverted sexual tendency. He considered that Wright was fit to plead to the indictment and to stand his trial.

This took place at St George's Hall, Liverpool on 11 June before Mr Justice Oliver, who twenty years before, in 1931, had appeared in that very same courtroom, defending William Herbert Wallace on a charge of murdering his wife, after establishing a complicated alibi. Although at first found guilty of murder, Wallace was eventually released by the Court of Appeal for lack of evidence. Oliver was a popular KC, considered to be an 'all-round man,' if somewhat straight-laced, and experienced in serious crime cases. He had been knighted and elevated to the bench in 1938, since when he had appeared in a number of notorious trials, including that of Allan Nunn May in 1946, convicted of passing information to the Russians.

Prosecuting Counsel, H.I. Nelson KC, opened the proceedings and outlined the case against the accused, which was to all intents and purposes open and shut. Wright had admitted on the Charge Sheet the correctness of the accusation against him and forensic evidence also linked the accused to the dead girl. Consultant Psychologist Charles Vaillant, who interviewed Wright whilst in prison, emphasised the fact that Wright had remained cold and detached throughout. 'You may think I am stupid,' Wright had said to him, 'but I believe that some evil spirit has taken possession of my body and the only way out is death.' Dr Vaillant told the court that Wright was an aggressive psychopath, but that this did not mean that he was insane. The jury took little time to produce a verdict of 'Guilty' and Wright was sentenced to death. He paid the final penalty for a pointless crime on Tuesday 3 July 1951.

12

DEATH OF A NIGHT WATCHMAN

Wythenshawe, population 66,000, has an area of eleven square miles and has been described as one of the largest housing estates in Europe. In 1951, parts of it were still being constructed, including the area then known as Crossacres, now Peel Hall, much of which was still open land. Work on this section had only just been started, roads were being laid out and sewers excavated in preparation for the building of houses. Dotted about the area were a number of night-watchmen's huts, usually crude corrugated iron structures, containing a few tools and a brazier to keep the watchman warm during his night shift. One such hut stood to the south of what is now Crossacres Junior School, by the side of Studland Road. The ground was open and unmade, and the area round the hut could become a quagmire whenever it rained.

This unprepossessing bit of land was the domain of George Camp, a fifty-eight-year-old, one-eyed labourer who was employed by the construction company to act as a night-watchman, which he did, with the help of his little mongrel dog, 'Peggy.' Camp was a secretive type, keeping very much to himself, but he could be found sometimes in the bar of the Red Lion at nearby Gatley or the Benchill Hotel on Hollyhedge Road, not far from the hut. The job called for little more than his presence on the site to prevent petty pilfering, although the watchmen had recently been warned that thefts of timber, lead and other building materials from the site compounds were rife and they had been asked to keep a special look-out for anyone getting too close to the stockpiled materials. Even so, it was highly likely that the watchmen never strayed far from the warmth of their braziers during the hours of darkness. Camp's hut, in which he passed most of his time when on shift, was completely hidden from Studland Road by mounds of earth thrown up by the excavations for sewers.

On Sunday 12 August 1951, at about 8.30 a.m., a bulldozer driver, William John Burke, discovered Camp's body lying inside his hut, feet towards the open door, his socks and boots covered in mud. The hut itself was littered with all sorts of rubbish, including bags of cement, bricks, drills and tools. The dead man had been very badly beaten. His jaw was fractured, as were several of his ribs and there were several marks on his head which appeared to have been made by an axe, which was lying on the floor and heavily bloodstained. By the side of the body was a heavy wooden plank, weighing about 48lb, which looked as though it might have been used to cause some of Camp's injuries.

Very soon, the police arrived in the person of Sergeant William Marshall, closely followed by Inspector Green, and the case was placed under the command of Detective Chief Superintendent Dan Timpany, head of the Manchester CID. Soon, police constables were frantically searching for clues, but despite the fact that the ground round the hut was very muddy, they found nothing in the way of footprints or any other pointers to the murderer, who seemed to have got clean away. A bulldozer driver, John Langrill, was able to say that he had seen George Camp at 3.45 p.m. on Saturday 11 August, which was when Camp had come on duty. He seemed to be in a normal frame of mind and there was nothing in his demeanour to draw attention to him. Langrill noticed that there was a fire in the brazier outside the hut, but a stove inside was unlit. Camp's dog, Peggy, had apparently bolted when her master was being attacked and was later found at Crossacres Farm, some distance away.

The Red Lion, Gatley, where George liked to drink. (© A. Hayhurst)

The murdered man's three brothers were amazed that George Camp had been assaulted and killed. 'He was a man with whom it was impossible to pick a quarrel,' Ben Camp said and went on to tell the police that George was something of a loner and was 'one of the best men you could meet.' Police enquiries disclosed that Camp had been seen talking to a young man in the Red Lion Hotel at Gatley on the previous Friday evening and issued a description, 'Aged about twenty-six, with fair hair and large hands, wearing a trench coat,' but nothing came of this. The 'young man' had either moved on or was keeping his head down, but so far, he was the only clue the police had got.

Meanwhile, the Home Office pathologist, George Bernard Manning, had examined the body, and it was clear that the night watchman had been subjected to a savage attack. Part of the report said:

The body was clothed in boots, socks, trousers, shirt, waistcoat, belt and braces. Laces of both boots were unfastened and trouser fly buttons undone apart from the top one. Second button from the top was missing and looked as if recently torn off. I discovered a similar button on the floor to the right of the body. There were two sacks full of cement, the top one of which was burst, allowing cement powder to fall round the head of the deceased. I discovered numerous blood splashes on the floor, walls and ceiling of the hut and on numerous articles inside. The only part of the hut walls that were free of blood was the inner right corner as I stood in the doorway looking in. There were also splashes of blood on the outside of the right-hand side of the hut as I faced the doorway. Also blood smears on the front wall and from one of those smears I removed some hairs, which I handed to DCI Green.

At 6 p.m. on the same day, I performed a post mortem at Platt Lane Police Mortuary. The body was that of a normally developed male aged about sixty, about 5ft 4' in height, left eyeball missing from its socket. It appeared to have been missing for some time. Right eye showed massive haemorrhages in the conjunctiva. There were contusions around both eyes and three small split wounds to the scalp. There was bruising all round these wounds and in my opinion, these three wounds could have been caused by a stick similar to pieces of wood produced, assuming they were in one piece. There were numerous recent abrasions on the body, on the back of both shoulders, on the back outside of the left arm and on the forehead. Also further abrasions on the left and right groins and an abrasion 3½' long and ½ inch wide running across the middle of the front leg. There was bruising on the face, especially on the left side and over the nose. The chest appeared to have undergone a severe compressed injury and 2nd to 11th ribs on the right hand side and from 2nd to 10th rib on the left hand side were all fractured in two places.

The metacarpals of middle and ring fingers on the left hand were fractured and the left ulna fractured just above the wrist. The lower jaw was fractured in two places on the right hand side, half an inch from the centre of the jaw and the nasal cartilage was fractured. The hyoid bone in the neck was fractured. The surface of the lungs was severely bruised and in my opinion, the group of fractures to the chest, nose and jaw could have been caused by something in the nature of Exhibit 6, [a wooden plank, weighing 48lb] being used as a weapon. The axe produced (Exhibit 7) could also have been used as a weapon and may have caused some of the injuries I found. The axe is fairly heavy and the injuries to the head would have required a moderate degree of force, but the injuries to the ribs would have required a very severe degree of force.

Deceased also had a rupture of the liver, resulting in haemorrhage of the abdominal cavity. This was due to the same blow, or blows which fractured the ribs. The injuries to the head were first sustained and after receiving these injuries, I consider that he would have been capable of sustaining physical movement, but not after receiving the wounds to the chest. My opinion is that the heavy plank either fell or was thrown on to the chest of the deceased and was the cause of death. In my opinion, death was due to shock and haemorrhage following multiple injuries to head and chest. I consider that death is likely to have taken place between 9 p.m. on 11 August and 3 a.m. on 12 August, 1951. [Estimating time of death is even today fraught with difficulty and many modern-day pathologists would hesitate about placing such rigid parameters]

A report from Albert Louis Allen, a Police Liaison Officer at the Forensic Science Laboratory at Preston, said that there was a large amount of blood on the floor and walls of the hut, which was all of Group O.

The watchman's hut. The lower part of George Camp's body can be seen just inside the door. (Courtesy of the National Archives)

The approximate site of the watchman's hut today. (© A. Hayhurst)

For the next few weeks, the police investigation looked like it was going nowhere. George Camp's savage attacker had left no clues whatsoever and had vanished into thin air, but on 8 October 1951, a prisoner at Strangeways Prison, Alfred Bradley, made an application to see the Governor, Gilbert Hair. The application was as a result of a conversation Bradley had had with the Church Army Captain, who regularly talked to the prisoners and who passed Bradley's request on to the Governor.

Bradley was taken to the Governor's office, where he appeared to be under great stress and in a highly emotional condition. He told the Governor that he had information about the murder of George Camp, placing great stress on the fact that although he had taken no part in the attack on the night-watchman, he had been there at the time.

It was not unusual for prisoners to make unfounded allegations and confessions whilst in prison, usually in the hope of getting a lighter or commuted sentence and Governor Hair was at first not convinced that Bradley was telling the truth. 'It's a serious offence to waste police time,' he told Bradley, 'and it might well land you in considerable trouble if you make a confession of murder in which there is no truth whatsoever.' Bradley insisted that he was telling the truth and that he was there at the hut with two other men, named Eric and Jock. When questioned further, Bradley admitted that he had hit Camp with a piece of wood and he offered to take the police to the scene, under guard.

Bradley was escorted back to his cell, whilst the Governor picked up the telephone and called Chief Superintendent Timpany, who arranged to visit the prison on the following day. Together with Chief Inspector Green, he confronted the prisoner and Timpany said, 'I understand that you have made verbal statements admitting that you are responsible for the murder of the watchman on a site at Wythenshawe.' Bradley answered in the affirmative. 'Do you understand that you may render yourself liable to be charged with murder?' the Superintendent said, looking straight at Bradley. 'Yes,' was the answer. 'I can only tell you the truth. It has played on my mind very much. I can only tell you that I was there and I will tell you what happened.' Following this, Bradley made a statement in which he described the two men who were with him. 'Eric,' he said, 'is tall with dark hair and Jock looks black round the chin when he has a shave. Jock is about 5ft 7in tall and aged about thirty.' Lowering his gaze to the floor, Bradley went on, 'I wouldn't like to say for certain, but I think they are funny men and both go in the Royal Brew Hotel.' Obtaining permission from the Governor, Timpany and Green took the prisoner to the Wythenshawe site, where Bradley identified the pub where he had first met the two men as the Benchill Hotel.

Three days later, Timpany visited the prison again and interviewed Bradley, telling him that the police were not satisfied that he was telling the truth about Eric and Jock. 'We have seen your father and two men named Eric and Jock, who are known in the Royal Brew Hotel.' said Timpany. 'Is the statement you made to us on 8 October true?' Bradley looked sheepish. 'You have seen them, have you? The part about myself is.'

'Which part is untrue?'

The part about Eric. There is no such person. Jock and I done it. I met him on the Friday evening and told him about George. I told him that George was living in a hut on the Estate and arranged to meet him in the 'Royal Brew' on the Saturday night, and to go to his hut to see if he had any money. Me and Jock got to the pub after closing time and I saw George outside. I spoke to him, then we went up to the hut in a car. I got out of the car and said to Jock, who was driving, 'It's about time you were going home.' He knew what I meant by that, as we had got it all planned to give Jock time to get to the hut and have a look round. I walked across with George but he saw Jock coming out of his hut. The old man went for him and Jock struck him. I fell in with Jock and did the same. When the old man fell down, I went back to the car and waited for Jock. Five minutes afterwards, he gave me some money and dropped me off in town.

This statement was completed at 4.12 p.m. but at 6.00 p.m., Bradley asked to make another statement, in which he said 'I did it on my own. No one was with me.' He now claimed to have been meeting Camp on a regular basis, when the watchman gave him money in return for sexual favours. On the night of the murder, he went to the hut with Camp, who made advances to him, which Bradley rejected and then launched a violent attack on the watchman. He was unclear as to the circumstances, due to the considerable amount of drink he had taken. Afterwards, he caught a bus to Manchester and got to London Road station, where he had a close look at the clothes he was wearing. His found that his overcoat was covered in blood and he cleaned it as best he could with a handkerchief. In the end, he left the coat at the Left Luggage office and went home. 'I'm sorry for what I've done,' he told the policemen, 'I didn't intend to kill.' When questioned further about the alleged indecency, he admitted that he had been doing this for many years, usually being paid for it, although Chief Inspector Green later said that he had made enquiries and so far as he had been able to find out, George Camp was not the sort of man that Alfred Bradley said he was.

The case was due to be heard on 27 November before Mr Justice Lynskey, but during the hearing, just as Bradley was taking the oath, the judge leaned forward and asked him to speak up, as it was vitally important that everyone in the courtroom should be able to hear him. Bradley showed no signs of having heard this stricture and the judge asked again, 'Do you understand?' Picking up the New Testament, Bradley threw it at the judge, shouting, 'I've finished.' After a short break, the trial proceeded, but at the end of the day's hearing, Mr Justice Lynskey announced that, as the jury might be influenced by Bradley's outburst, he considered that he had no alternative but to pronounce a mistrial.

On 6 December, the second trial started in front of Mr Justice Stable and the evidence was presented to a new jury. Bradley's own statement was read out, accusing George Camp of being a homosexual and claiming that he was sorry for what he had done. He had had no intention of hitting out and had done so in disgust at the other man's approaches. 'Money can get people into trouble,' he had said. 'Money and drink.'

The jury were almost certainly influenced by the description of George Camp's horrendous injuries, which could only have been done during a frenzied attack. The defence, led by Kenneth Burke KC claimed that Camp's death could have been an accident. If Camp had been knocked to the ground in the first part of the struggle, the heavy plank could have fallen inadvertently and crushed him. An alternative line was that the attack had been provoked by Camp's behaviour and therefore, the charge should be reduced to one of manslaughter.

The trial took two days, at the end of which the verdict was 'Guilty.' An appeal on the grounds of insanity was refused and on Tuesday 15 January 1952, Albert Pierrepoint and Robert L. Stewart carried out the sentence of the court.

13

THE SHATTERED
BOTTLES MURDER

Miles Platting, 1962

Number 162 Hulme Hall Lane, Miles Platting, was a small corner shop, with living accommodation above it, run by fifty-seven-year-old Sarah Isabella Cross. She received occasional help from her husband, David Henry, who had a full-time job during the day as a powder sprayer. The shop was an end of terrace property, on the corner of Hulme Hall Lane and Iron Street, with windows facing both. The side wall of the house, facing Iron Street, bore several advertising boards, as did the Hulme Hall frontage, with two suspended advertisements for Players cigarettes over the entrance door. Inside the rather cramped shop, Mrs Cross sold sweets, tobacco, soft drinks and ice cream and the average weekly turnover was about £80, of which £12 was taken on a Friday, the busiest day of the week.

David and Sarah led a very ordered life and the routine in the shop was followed religiously. Each day, after the shop closed, the daily takings were taken upstairs to be counted, leaving only a 10s float in the till, always comprising two two-shilling pieces, six sixpenny pieces, 2s in pennies and 1s in halfpennies. Hidden away under the counter, for 'emergencies' were a 10s note and 10s in silver.

On the morning of Friday 4 May 1962, David Cross left for work at 6.30 a.m., leaving his wife in bed, as was usual. He did not come home for lunch and was normally away until about 6 o'clock. During the day, Sarah busied herself in the back living room (lounge) on the ground floor and when someone came into the shop, a bell would ring and she would go into the shop to serve the customer. There was a small counter, under which were kept bottles of soft drinks and mineral water and, at the rear of the serving area, another unit with a built-in till had bottles of milk stored beneath. The days of refrigerated cabinets had not yet arrived in Hulme Hall Lane! The till was also fitted with a bell, which rang whenever it was

No. 162 Hulme Hall Lane, Miles Platting. (Courtesy of the National Archives)

opened and both shop and till bells could be heard clearly in the living room, from which a door led into a scullery, which in turn gave access to the back yard, the door to which was always kept barred. The only lavatory was in the yard.

At 4.25 p.m., the shop bell rang and Mrs Cross greeted Peter Mallard, who was employed as a van guard by the cigarette firm Gallaghers and who knew the Crosses well. 'Afternoon Peter,' Mrs Cross said cheerfully, as she accepted delivery of two cartons of cigarettes, signing the delivery sheet that served as a receipt. Mallard answered her greeting and then left. The transaction had taken barely a minute.

At 4.45 p.m., schoolgirl Stephanie Lesley Howarth aged nine, boarded a No. 65 bus to the Playhouse Theatre and then a No. 53. She was going to see her married sister, Doreen Kenyon, who ran a hairdresser's shop at 182 Hulme Hall Lane, ten doors away from the tobacconist's. Within minutes, Stephanie came out of her sister's shop, a few pennies in her hand, and walked down to Mrs Cross's shop, with the intention of buying some chocolate from 'Aunty Belle.' The shop door was closed, but she opened it and went in. There was no one else in the shop at this time and although she heard the shop bell ring as she opened the door, no one came to serve her. This was unusual, as Sarah Cross was usually very much on the ball when it came to serving customers and relieving them of their money. The chocolate on which the young girl had her eye was in a glass case and she walked over to it and tapped on it. Still, no one came and this time, she went to the ice cream display and tapped again. Beginning to feel a little impatient, the girl went to the counter and looked over it. To her horror, she saw Mrs Cross's feet, complete with slippers, on the floor, although she could not see anything else as she was not tall enough. Running out of the shop, she went back to her sister, screaming for help.

Doreen Kenyon, together with her assistant, Joan Taylor, hurried the short distance to the shop and saw Sarah Cross lying on the floor behind the counter. Her feet were facing towards the inside door leading to the living quarters and she was lying on her left side. Her arms were straight up over her head and there were scratches and blood on her arms. Lifting the flap, the two women hurried behind the counter and saw that Sarah Cross's head was obscured by her overall and they struggled to free it. For some reason, it would not come free and during their efforts, Doreen heard a gurgling sound which she thought came from the recumbent figure. Stepping back hastily, she saw that there was broken glass all over the floor and round the body and a pool of what she thought was mineral water.

Doreen's assistant, after seeing the body, left the shop and went to 149 Hulme Hall Lane, where George Howard kept a general store and sub-post office. This was opposite the tobacconists and Howard hurried across the road and went in. He bent down and got hold of Sarah Cross's wrist, feeling for a pulse, but could not find one, although the body was still warm. He also was unable to free the overall from the dead woman's head and, apart from the broken glass, he noticed several pennies by her shoulder. This was to be an important part of the case later on.

Returning to the entrance door of the shop, he saw an ambulance approaching and flagged it down, waving his arms wildly. He ran towards the ambulance and as he did so, the shop door slammed shut and he heard the Yale lock slip. Hurriedly, he explained the situation to the two ambulance men, who left their vehicle and attempted to enter the shop door, which would not open. Realising what had happened to the lock, George Howard launched a mighty kick at it and the door flew back, crashing against the wall of the shop. As he went behind the counter, he noticed that the till was open.

Between the three men, they managed to bring Mrs Cross's body to the front of the counter and when they had moved it, they saw more coins that had been under the body. Howard then went outside to await the arrival of the police and by the time he went back into the shop, ambulance driver James Dawson had been able to free the overall and could see that there were several lacerations on the woman's skull and there was a large amount of congealed blood inside the overall. He, too, felt for a pulse unsuccessfully. As Mrs Cross's body was moved, he saw a small knife on the floor.

Just then, another ambulance arrived and Dawson went into the scullery to clean his hands. As he went through the lounge, he noticed a bureau against the wall, the lid of which was open and a small drawer was sticking out. It looked to him as though someone had been going through the contents. Both lounge and scullery door into the back yard were open. The body was put into the second ambulance and taken to Ancoats Hospital, where Sarah Cross was pronounced dead.

The shop floor after the murder. Note the broken glass and loose coins. (Courtesy of the National Archives)

That evening, Charles Arthur St Hill, Home Office pathologist for Liverpool and the North West, performed the post-mortem. St Hill had appeared in many notorious cases and was to be involved with the Moors murders a few years later. He was an honorary fellow of the Association of Forensic Medicine and also director of the sub-department of forensic medicine at Liverpool University. His report, at the National Archives, states that 'I found the body of a well-nourished woman, 5ft 6' tall. She was fully clothed except that there were no shoes on the feet. The upper part of the clothing was bloodstained but did not appear to have been disturbed.'

On the head and neck, the pathologist found a gaping laceration of the right scalp, about 3½in above the right ear and there were other wounds and considerable bruising. There was also a 9in fracture of the skull running from the right ear. The bones of the face and the front of the skull had been widely separated from the rest of the skull. There were also other scratches and marks on the trunk, arms and hands, which had probably been caused by an attempt to ward off the blows, which were heavy ones. The cause of death was attributed to cerebral contusion and haemorrhage due to the skull fracture, which Dr Hill thought had been caused by a bottle or similar object, although he qualified this by saying that an empty bottle would have been unlikely to have caused the major injuries. In Dr Hill's opinion, he expected that there would be blood on the clothing of the assailant and also on the shoes.

The police investigation was started by Chief Inspector Clifford Haigh, who was called to the murder scene at 5.20 p.m. By this time, the body had been removed and he remarked on the large quantity of broken glass on the floor, behind the counter and the sum of 9s 1½d in coins. He counted five bottle tops, with the corks intact and a quantity of broken ice-cream cones on the floor near the entrance to the lounge. Examining the shop till, he noted that the top edge was splintered and on opening the drawer fully, he found 3s in coin.

Inspector Trevor Green, a fingerprint expert with twenty-two years experience, visited the shop and along the edge of the door that led from the lounge into the scullery, he found one complete fingerprint and part of two others. The door had been newly painted and the fingerprints were embedded in the paint. These fingerprints were soon traced to twenty-five-year-old James Smith, who was born in Edinburgh. James Smith's home life had been happy enough, although the family were very poor and his few friends found him to be shy and a poor mixer. Leaving school at fifteen, having been an average scholar, he had a succession of poorly paid jobs, then three years in the Army, at the end of which his conduct was described as 'Very Good' and his Army reference said, 'Gunner Smith is an intelligent and well turned out young soldier. He has been employed as a Battery Motor Transport Clerk and has worked well. With a little more ambition, Smith would go far in the Army.' He eventually ended up in Manchester in 1959, employed as a rubber moulder, earning £16 a week. From demob out of the Army in March 1957 to the time of his arrest, Smith had had no fewer than eleven different jobs.

He married in 1958: his wife bringing to the marriage her two children and they now also had a seven-month-old baby. Smith had a police record as far back as 1950, having been in and out of the courts for minor offences, the latest of which was on 15 July. In 1961 he was up before Manchester Magistrates accused of receiving stolen property, for which he was fined £5.

Smith's wife, born Mary Townsley, was also Scottish and had a police record. She was actively engaged in prostitution and between June 1951 and October 1956, was six times cautioned for loitering and importuning. She had three illegitimate children prior to marrying Smith, one of whom died when only one day old. Her list of offences was more than twice as long as her husband's and they were now living at 4 Corfe Street, Beswick, in a small rented house, where the police eventually caught up with him.

In the meantime, the police had also started to interview every young man in the Miles Platting area and Barry V —, then a territorial soldier on camp in Warwickshire, was surprised and not a little disturbed to be told to report to the Guard Room where a policeman was waiting to interview him about the murder. He had, of course, nothing to tell the police, having no connection at all with the case, other than living in the Miles Platting area, and he was soon released back to his

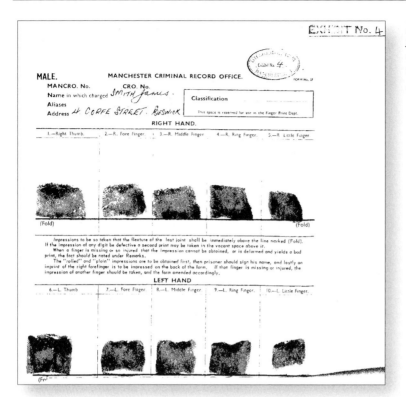

Army duties. Forty-six years later, he happened to be waiting to use the photocopier at Manchester Central Library, when he saw coming off the machine a newspaper page with the headline, 'Broken-Glass Clue to Shop Murder,' and there followed a conversation with the author, to whom he told this little story.

At 8 a.m. on Sunday morning, 27 May, Detective Superintendent Eric Cunningham, together with DI Butcher and DS Dodsworth, went to 4 Corfe Street and knocked on the door. Ten minutes later, they were still knocking, the sound of which was now arousing the neighbourhood from its Sunday-morning slumbers. Suddenly, the door flew open and a rather dishevelled Mary Smith appeared. Briefly explaining why they were there, the policemen went into the house and saw James Smith in the front room. DS Cunningham spoke first, telling Smith who they were and then said, 'Are you James Smith who was born in Edinburgh in 1936?'

'Yes,' replied Smith.

'What's to do? Are you in regular employment?' asked Cunningham.

'Yes, I work in Failsworth.'

'Were you working there on Friday May 4?'

There was a pause and then, 'Yes. I would be on days that week.'

'What time did you finish work?'

'Twelve o'clock. We finish early on Fridays.'

'Do you know Hulme Hall Lane?'

Another hesitation and then, 'I know of Hulme Hall Lane and I know what you are on about. When I heard you knocking, I knew who it was. I lay there for ten minutes listening to you.'

'Do you know the shop at 162 Hulme Hall Lane?'

'Where the woman was killed? Everybody round here knows that. It's been on the television and in the newspapers.' The atmosphere in the small front room was tense as Cunningham went on. 'Have you ever been in that shop?'

'Never in my life. I've passed it, that's all.'

'Were you anywhere near that shop on Friday, May 4?'

'I walked past it on my way home' Smith replied. When asked if he usually went that way, he said, 'No. If I come that way at all, I go to Stevenson Square and get a trolley bus.' Superintendent Cunningham stared hard at Smith. 'I believe that you have been in that shop and I think you were in the shop on 4 May.

'I ought to know,' protested Smith and then stood silent whilst the Superintendent cautioned him. 'I am taking you into custody and you will be charged with murder.'

Smith looked sullen. 'You don't expect me to say anything, do you?' he said, before being taken to Mill Street police station and locked up. Inspector Butcher then went through the house and took possession of various items of clothing and personal effects.

Later the same day, Smith was again interviewed and his first words when the police entered his cell were, 'I suppose somebody saw me drunk outside the shop.' He admitted that he had been drinking after leaving work on the Friday. 'I was at the Sun Inn,' he told the police, 'near work, until ten past three with three mates. Then I went for a haircut with one of them, Ken Wrigley.' (According to Wrigley's own statement, he and Smith went for a haircut before going to the pub and Wrigley left the Sun Inn at 2 p.m. leaving Smith still there drinking.)

A workmate, Edward Hunt, remembered Smith and Wrigley coming into the Sun Inn and his estimate of the amount of beer that Smith drink before Hunt left at 2.50 p.m. was four to five pints. The landlord, Alfred Blakely, saw him come into the pub a little before 1 p.m. with another man (presumably Wrigley) and last saw him just before 2.45 p.m., when he had been served with three pints of bitter. He was adamant that Smith had not had enough drink to make him intoxicated.

The interview continued, 'The insurance man saw me at home at half-past four, when you say it happened.' Cunningham looked at him sharply. 'I haven't mentioned any time.' Smith seemed unperturbed. 'It's been in all the papers,' was his reply.

Smith was then offered the chance to make a statement, putting his side of the case, but he declined. 'It's your case,' he said, 'I'm saying no more.' When cautioned yet again, he said, 'Nothing to say whatsoever.' Later, when being questioned further, Cunningham said, 'Perhaps I ought to tell you that your fingerprint impressions were found on the premises. You say you have never been there.' 'I'm not interested in what you've got,' Smith shot back. 'I was home after 3.30 p.m. anyway.'

The police were now in possession of Smith's clothing, including a pair of blue jeans with a leather belt, a blue shirt and a blue donkey jacket, together with a pair of black brogue shoes. They had also found a green check shirt at Smith's house, which was soaking in a bowl of water. In addition, the police found a single-breasted jacket, in which were a torch, a pair of wire cutters, a pair of long-nosed pliers, a penknife and an electrical screwdriver. Smith was now fingerprinted, after which Dr Kerr took two samples of blood from the accused man and comment was made about several scars and scratches on his hands, which appeared to be of recent origin. All the items taken from the house, including the clothes Smith was wearing when arrested, were sent to the Forensic Science laboratory at Preston for further examination.

Meanwhile, Chief Inspector Albert Louis Allen had been carefully collecting every fragment of glass from the murder scene and from the clothing of the dead woman. The scientists at Preston were asked to be equally zealous in looking for any fragments of glass, however small, from the items they had received. Further witnesses were interviewed including a twenty-seven-year-old housewife, Kathleen Wilds, who was friendly with Smith's wife and who used to visit her regularly at Corfe Street. She had been asked by Mary Smith to give evidence on Smith's behalf and had agreed to go to a solicitor, where she gave a statement saying that she had been at 4 Corfe Street at five-past four on the afternoon of the murder and that James Smith was at home at that time. She also said that she had stayed at the house for ten minutes and had then left, James Smith still being there.

A week before the trial was due to begin, Kathleen Wilds could stand the strain no longer and went to Inspector Butcher and told him that her statement at the solicitors was untrue from beginning to end. She now explained that she had only made it because she was afraid of Mary Smith, who had threatened to cut her with a razor if she did not say what she was told. She admitted that she could not remember where she was on the day of the murder and a new statement was taken.

The insurance man who Smith had said saw him at home on the afternoon of the murder was traced. His name was John Hamilton and what he had to tell the police was not too helpful. Although he said that he usually visited the Smiths on Friday afternoons between 4.30 and 5 p.m., to collect the premiums of 9s 1½d, he could not be certain that he had actually visited 4 Corfe Street on Friday 4 May. 'It might,' he told the police 'possibly have been on the following day, as my records do not show the actual dates I receive premiums from clients.' However, a hand-written addendum to his typewritten statement said that it was his almost invariable practice to visit on Fridays and it was probable that it had been on Friday 4 May. The statement did not say whether or not he had seen James Smith, whatever the day he had called.

According to Mary Smith, she had had a short conversation with Hamilton about the Cup Final, which was Tottenham against Burnley (Tottenham won 3-1) and had told him that her husband was not interested in football. Hamilton had replied that 'It's a poor sort of Scotsman who is not interested in football,' whereupon she had shouted to her husband, who was in the kitchen, 'Did you hear that, Jimmy?' and Smith had replied, 'I'm a good one.' The insurance man insisted that he could not remember any such conversation taking place, but as he made nearly 700 calls every week and admitted that he did usually chat to his clients about events of the day, this is perhaps not surprising.

After the committal proceedings at the Magistrate's Court, Smith was sent to Liverpool Assizes to be tried. The trial opened at St George's Hall, in front of Mr Justice Stable, with Glyn Burrell QC prosecuting and Godfrey Heilpern QC and W.F.N. Percy acting for the defence. The prosecution emphasised that this was a case of capital murder, in other words murder in the furtherance of theft. This was shown by Mr Cross's evidence of the likely takings by 4.30 on Friday afternoons (he said that the usual amount would have been about £6), the scattering of cash on the shop floor and evidence of blood smears on the bureau in the lounge, which had been opened. It was also evident that a struggle took place behind the counter and strands of hair and roots had been found, torn from the dead woman's head. Nothing of any significance had been found on the dead woman's clothing, but a fingerprint had been found on the door leading from the lounge to the kitchen and Mr Burrell emphasised the finding of glass in the accused man's clothing and at his home.

Inspector Green, in his evidence, said that there were sixteen points of comparison between the fingerprint on the door and Smith's left middle finger. Three other prints had been found, but had not been admitted in evidence as they did not have the necessary sixteen points. The significance of the fingerprints was that the accused said that he had never been in the premises. If he had been in the shop and the print had also been in the shop itself, it would have had little value as evidence, 'But here,' Glyn Burrell said, with a flourish, 'It is in the living quarters of the premises, premises which he says he has passed and did pass on the 4 May, and into which he has never ventured.'

Evidence from the Director of the North Western Forensic Science Laboratory, Emlyn Glyndwr Davies, showed that there was no evidence of sexual attack on Mrs Davies and that the many blood stains on the premises were of Group O. (This was the blood group of both Mrs Cross and the accused man, but approximately 47 per cent of the population are Group O, so it was inconclusive). On 27 May, Davies had visited the Corfe Street premises and in the back bedroom, he had examined a chair cushion and found four fragments of glass, plus a further fragment on the left hand front of the chair. When Smith's clothing was examined, he found a number of bloodstains, some of which gave a positive reaction for human blood, but due to the age of the stains, the result of grouping tests were inconclusive. Further pieces of glass were obtained from the dead woman's clothing and on the carpet.

The major piece of evidence, however, damning though the fingerprint was, came in the shape of five glass mineral-water bottles that Chief Inspector Allen had spent many laborious hours gluing together.' They stood on a table, in the well of the court, objects of curiosity for all in the courtroom. 'It was,' said Mr Burrell, 'a truly remarkable piece of work, insofar as Chief Inspector Allen has been able to fit very small pieces into position and substantially build up the shapes of the five bottles. The inspector had taken comparison photographs, which the defence had tried to have disallowed at the Magistrate's Court, but without success. Judge Stable now gave permission for one reconstituted bottle to be destroyed for examination jointly by prosecution and defence. Of the five very small pieces of glass that had been found at Smith's home, one had made an excellent fit with a piece of glass found in the shop. The other pieces were in turn able to be fitted into bottles which had essentially been reassembled by the inspector. Not only did the pieces fit, but the markings on the fractured surfaces also matched completely. Some thousands of pieces had been collected and it had taken the Chief Inspector more than 200 painstaking hours to reassemble them. To add to the evidence, experts from Sheffield University carried out density tests and chemical analysis on the pieces of glass in question, which confirmed Chief Inspector Allen's findings.

It had been the intention of the defence to put forward the alibi that Smith had been at home with his wife and daughter at the time of the murder, but in view of Kathleen Wilds' new evidence, this was now no longer possible. A medical history was prepared by the splendidly named Dr Northage J. de V. Mather, a consultant psychiatrist, whilst Smith was in Strangeways awaiting trial, but this offered little help to the defence. Although his uncle was said to have been admitted to a mental institution some sixty years ago, he was later released, married and lived to the age of seventy-five. The report said:

> Smith was an astute, keenly attentive man, of good average intelligence and with a full apprehension of his predicament. An E.C.G. test was within normal limits. During the course of our conversations, Smith admitted that the fingerprint was his and that he had probably been in the shop on another occasion, which he has forgotten. He was adamant that the print did not refer to the incident on 4 May, although his explanation did not explain how the fingerprint happened to be on a door in the house part of the premises, to which customers would normally have had no access.

Dr Mather was unable to find that Smith was anything but normal and there was no question of insanity.

The trial extended over three days, mainly because of the technical evidence of the glass bottles, and the jury had no problem in bringing in a verdict of 'Guilty.' The death penalty for certain classes of murder had been rescinded at this time, but murder in the course of theft was not one of them and Mr Justice Stable donned the black cap before pronouncing sentence. Afterwards, he expressed his appreciation of the excellent work done by Chief Inspector Allen and also the staff at the Forensic Science Laboratory.

An appeal on 8 November was swiftly turned down and Smith walked to the gallows at 8 a.m. on Wednesday 28 November 1962, where Harry Allen helped him to atone for a senseless and brutal murder.

BIBLIOGRAPHY

1. A MULTIPLE TRAGEDY
The Annual Register
Manchester Courier & Lancashire General Advertiser
Manchester Daily Examiner

2. THE MANCHESTER MARTYRS
HO 45/7799
Doughty, Jack *The Manchester Outrage – A Fenian Tragedy* (Jade Publishing, 2001)
Glyn, Anthony *High Upon the Gallows Tree* (Anvil Books, 1967)
O'Dea, John *The Story of the Old Faith in Manchester* (R. & T. Washbourne Ltd, 1910)
Ramon, Marta *A Provisional Dictator: James Stephens and the Fenian Movement* (UCD Press, 2007)
Rose, Paul *The Manchester Martyrs – A Fenian Tragedy* (Lawrence & Wishart, 1970)

3. 'FOR THAT I DON...'
P.COM. 8/108
Fielding, Steve The *Hangman's Record* Vol. 1 (Chancery House Press, 1994)
Manchester City News
Sheffield Daily Telegraph
Ward, David *King of the Lags* (Elec Books Ltd, 1963)

4. THE ASHTON POISONING CASE
QEV/15 (Lancashire Record Office)
Berry, James *My Experiences as an Executioner* (Percy Lund & Co, *c.* 1900)
Evans, Stewart P. *Executioner: The Chronicles of James Berry* (Sutton Publishing, 2004)
Ashton Reporter
Cheshire Ancestor (The Journal of the Family History Society of Cheshire) (2008)

5. THE STRANGEWAYS MURDER

ASSI 52/10

Anon 'The Strangeways Murder' *The Sporting News*, 1888 (Facsimile published by
  Clifford Elmer Books Ltd)

Oldham Standard

6. A NASTY SHOCK!

Ashton Reporter

7. MURDERED FOR 18 PENCE

ASSI 52/130

Manchester Evening News

8. DEATH OF A SHOPKEEPER

ASSI 52/203

HO 144/17280++

HO 144/17281 *

PCOM 8/335++

Manchester Courier

Oldham Standard

9. DEATH IN CARRS WOOD

ASSI 52/350

HO 144/3839++

MEPO 3/1593

PCOM 8/14

Manchester Evening News

Manchester Guardian

Stockport Advertiser

10. 'HELLO TISH'

ASSI 86/43++

DPP 2/2008++

PCOM 9/1579

PCOM 9/1773

Fielding, Steve *Pierrepoint: A Family of Executioners* (John Blake, 2006)

Eddleston, John J. *Murderous Manchester* (Breedon Books, 1997)

Pierrepoint, Albert *Executioner: Pierrepoint* (Harrap, 1974)

Empire News

Evening Express

Empire News

11. MURDER ON IMPULSE
ASSI 52/732
ASSI 86/69 ++
DPP 52/732
HO 45/25683
PCOM 9/1594

12. DEATH OF A NIGHT WATCHMAN
ASSI 52/714
ASSI 86/53 ++
DPP 2/2107
PCOM 9/1495
Manchester Evening News

13. THE SHATTERED BOTTLES MURDER
ASSI 52/1262
DPP 2/3478

* = Redacted version of file released.
++ = Freed under Freedom of Information Act, 2000.

INDEX